To Bradley, I love your Mom — cook for her. SWS

Happy cooking! Sallie Swor

You're Grown—
Now You Can Cook

Cooking for Everyone – Kitchen Novice to Gourmet Genius

SALLIE STAMPS SWOR

You're Grown—Now You Can Cook

by Sallie Stamps Swor

ISBN 978-1-63393-477-1

Published by

 köehlerbooks™

210 60th Street
Virginia Beach, VA 23451
800-435-4811
www.koehlerbooks.com

DEDICATION

To my son Richard, who keeps my world full of music and laughter.

And to my husband Sammy, who may not be the most adventurous eater but who never fails to believe in me, even when I'm just plain silly.

I can't leave out my sister Mary, who absolutely put her foot down and made me publish this book by promising me a party, or my Mother, my original cooking guru.

It is also dedicated to my very wonderful and patient friends who were my tasters, testers, prep chefs, and support group. You know who you are! xo

Table of Contents

TABLE OF CONTENTS

About the Cookbook

Originally I wrote this cookbook at my son's request. He had moved into a first apartment with a completely unstocked kitchen, a healthy appetite, and the desire to eat well without spending a ridiculous amount of time or money. His friends were delighted by the dinners he prepared, and soon they all wanted copies of his cookbook. My friends, many of whom are very accomplished cooks, began requesting copies as well, and so here it is: *You're Grown—Now You Can Cook.*

This cookbook is designed for the person who wants to cook and would like directions that spell out everything you need to know about the recipe: the ingredients and where to get them, the equipment needed, and exactly what to do in the kitchen. The recipes are concise, making the dishes a breeze to produce in a home kitchen. Directions are listed in steps rather than paragraph form so they are easier to read. All recipes include helpful hints, instructions, serving suggestions, tips about where to find products in the grocery store, and even ideas for easy cleanup. Menu planning and party ideas are also included along with informative and entertaining text that makes reading this cookbook fun. Techniques are thoroughly explained for the novice chef. Most importantly, the recipes will allow you to cook for yourself, friends, and family knowing the results will always be delicious.

All the recipes in this book have been tried and approved by my son and our friends and family. I have loved collecting our favorites, creating new ones, and writing these recipes in a way that will make them simple to follow and the results a joy to eat. Confidence in your kitchen and compliments at the table are a guarantee with this cookbook.

You're Grown—Now You Can Cook is the ultimate cookbook for anyone who loves good food and wants to master the kitchen. It's a perfect book for a high school or college graduate, new apartment dweller or homeowner, newlyweds, or those who would like to expand their cooking skills. This cookbook is great for the novice cook but will be enjoyed by anyone who loves good food, great recipes, finds joy in cooking. The recipes in this cookbook are destined to become favorites and the cook is guaranteed be a star in the kitchen. These are recipes you'll be making the rest of your life!

My website, based on this cookbook, includes a frequently updated blog, may be found at: thedeerone.com/wordpress

Enjoy!

INTRODUCTION TO
Appetizers

I love this section of the cookbook. Appetizers are such an essential part of entertaining. When friends come to visit, a yummy bite of something in hand makes everyone feel just a little more at home. The word "appetizer" means food and drink to stimulate the appetite. Doesn't that sound just right?

These recipes are all easy to prepare, and making two or three appetizers could be the menu for an entire party. Sometimes it's a lot more fun to wander around nibbling something delicious than to sit down at the table. Whether you plan to base a party on appetizers, or just pick one to serve before dinner, you'll find something perfect from these recipes.

SOME THINGS TO KNOW ABOUT APPETIZERS

- » Count on 3 to 4 small one-bite appetizers per person if you are serving them before dinner. You really need only one type of appetizer if dinner is to follow.
- » If your appetizer is the meal, or maybe you're going to serve appetizers at a cocktail or tea party, then double that number. Remember most guys eat more—at least mine do, so think about your guest list and plan accordingly.
- » If you are serving a meal, one type of appetizer is plenty, and it is okay to run out. You want your guests to eat your dinner! Try to stick to appetizers that don't require a plate or silverware if they are to be served before dinner. That way you won't spend hours doing dishes after guests have left.

EASIEST APPETIZERS IF YOU ARE PRESSED FOR TIME

- » Think grocery store salad bar—olives, marinated vegetables, peppers, and precut vegetables for a purchased dip.
- » Hummus with crackers and veggies. (Hummus recipe, page 17)
- » Cheese—one or two varieties with crackers. Add chutney or pepper jelly to be a rock star. (Check out the recipe for Fondue without the Pot recipe, page 18.)
- » Nuts *(Hint: Heat for about 15 seconds in the microwave to bring out flavors. Drop in dried rosemary if you have any.)*
- » Popcorn—page 22 is completely dedicated to it!
- » Good chips and salsa are readily available. (Pico de Gallo recipe, page 23)

Some of the appetizers in this book are easy to double and freeze, like Spinach Balls, which is especially handy if the party is more impromptu. Something homemade that you can pull out of the freezer and serve twenty minutes later with absolutely minimal effort is just delightful.

Appetizers to ignore include: overpriced frozen items from the grocery store that end in the suffix "tizer," salty prepared snack mixes, and frozen fried foods, just to name a few.

BLT Dip

This is a perfect dip for tailgating or entertaining at home. Serve with toasted bread cut in squares or bagel chips and lettuce leaves so people can make their own little open-face sandwiches and wraps. So yummy and so easy!

INGREDIENTS

10 pieces bacon, cooked and crumbled *see note

¾ cup mayonnaise (the kind made with olive oil is healthier)

¾ cup sour cream

2 tomatoes, chopped (grocery store salad bar, about a cup)

1 tbsp vinegar **see note

1 tbsp sugar

1 tsp salt

½ tsp pepper

For serving: toasted bread cut in squares, or bagel chips, and lettuce leaves to make wraps

DIRECTIONS

Mix everything together and taste for seasoning.

Makes about 2½ cups

*Bacon can be cooked in a large skillet over medium-high heat or cooked in the microwave in a micro-wave-safe dish lined with paper towels. You can also purchase pre-cooked bacon that you microwave for about a minute. I'm not a big fan, but I guess it would do in a pinch.

**You can use lemon juice if you don't have vinegar.

Blue Cheese and Caramelized Onion Dip

Is this really worth the (small) effort when you can purchase a variety of dips at the grocery store? You can count on it. People go nuts for this dip. It's about a million times better than anything you can buy pre-made. Serve this with a good old bag of potato chips and you'll get compliments beyond your wildest dreams. I always have to double the recipe. This is a tradition at our Super Bowl Party, and if I didn't serve it, I think people might actually leave. Oh well, better to be loved for your dip making skills than not loved at all!

INGREDIENTS

1 tbsp vegetable oil

1 cup green onions, thinly sliced (grocery store salad bar)

½ tsp each salt and sugar

¾ cup mayonnaise (the kind made with olive oil is healthier)

¾ cup sour cream

4 oz crumbled blue cheese

For serving: your favorite chips

DIRECTIONS

Heat oil in heavy medium-sized saucepan over medium-low heat.

Add green onions. Sprinkle with salt and sugar.

Cook until onions are golden brown (caramelized), stirring occasionally, about 20 minutes. Cool.

Mix together mayonnaise and sour cream in a medium bowl.

Add the blue cheese and mash it up a little.

Stir in caramelized onions.

Check seasonings and season to taste with salt and pepper as needed.

Makes about 2 cups

Suggestion: Best if you cover dip and refrigerate until flavors blend, about 2 hours. You could keep leftovers for a day. I've never had any!

Serving Suggestion: This is also really good as a topping for a hamburger or turkey burger.

Bruschetta with Tomato Topping

I recently served this to a friend who travels all over the world and dines in fabulous restaurants. She said (I'm not kidding), "This may be the absolute best thing I've ever eaten." Then she amended that to, "No, this IS the best thing I've ever eaten." Better try it and see!

INGREDIENTS

1 loaf French or Italian bread, sliced diagonally into ¾ inch slices

4 tbsp melted butter

½ tsp garlic salt

TOPPING

14.5 oz can diced tomatoes, undrained (fire-roasted tomatoes are fine.)

2 cloves garlic, chopped (you can use garlic in a jar)

2 tbsp sugar

2 tbsp red wine vinegar or apple cider vinegar

1 tsp salt

¼ tsp red pepper flakes

For serving: cheese of choice, Brie, Parmesan, Blue, Gruyere

DIRECTIONS

Make the topping. In a saucepan combine all topping ingredients except cheese.

Boil over medium heat, reduce to simmer, and cook until thickened, stirring occasionally for about 20 minutes.

Remove from heat and taste for salt. (It should have a salty-sweet taste.)

Preheat the oven to 350 degrees.

Mix melted butter, and garlic salt together, and brush on bread, or dip one side of bread into the melted butter.

Place bread, buttered side up, on a baking sheet, and bake for 10 minutes. *(hint: Line baking sheet with aluminum foil for easy cleanup.)*

You may want to broil the toasts for a minute to brown the tops, and if you do, keep an eye on the toasts so they don't burn.

Top each toast with a spoon of warm tomato topping and a small slice of cheese.

Makes about 1½ cups of tomato topping

Suggestion: This tomato topping is equally delicious cold. It keeps for about a week, so it's a great instant snack or appetizer. It's wonderful on grilled or broiled fish and chicken.

Butter Bean Hummus

In Atlanta, I discovered that hummus can be made with almost any bean. A restaurant there served a butter bean hummus, and I couldn't wait to get in my own kitchen and reproduce it. Now I've made hummus with lots of different ingredients. Maybe the most creative yet was boiled peanuts, which was delicious but took more time because the peanuts had to be shelled. It certainly delighted my Georgia friends! This is still our family's favorite hummus. You can whip up this appetizer in under five minutes and charm everyone with something that is just a little off the beaten path. The vegetables make a beautiful presentation.

INGREDIENTS

1 can butter beans, well drained (approximately 15 oz can; varies by brand)

1 clove garlic

2 tbsp tahini (found in the Asian foods section of the grocery store)

2 tbsp olive oil, plus 1 tsp for drizzling on top

Juice of ½ lemon

½ tsp salt

⅛ tsp cayenne pepper

For serving: any or all of the following: pita bread or chips, mixed olives, celery, radishes, carrot chips, and cucumber slices

DIRECTIONS

Combine all ingredients in a food processor or blender until very smooth.

Taste for seasonings.

Put hummus in a small serving dish and drizzle the top with about 1 tsp of olive oil.

Makes about 1½ cups

Serving Suggestion: This is beautiful served in a bowl in the middle of a plate surrounded by the chips and veggies of your choice.

Suggestion: This recipe is versatile and can be made with other beans. Experiment with navy beans, garbanzo beans, edamame—really any bean you like. Leftovers keep for several days in the refrigerator. Cover well or store in a plastic container.

Fondue Without the Pot

Pull this out of the hat after a movie or concert for a late night supper or snack. It's genius—easy and sophisticated; perfect for date night because you can assemble everything ahead of time and cook it when you're ready. This recipe is very easy to halve for a smaller group.

INGREDIENTS

1 lb Fontina or Gruyere cheese

4 garlic cloves, thinly sliced

2 tbsp olive oil

1 tsp Italian seasoning (or a combination of basil and oregano)

1 tsp salt

1 tsp pepper

1 loaf French or Italian bread

DIRECTIONS

Position the oven rack about 5 inches from the heat source and turn the oven on to broil.

Let it preheat for five minutes.

Cut cheese into 1-inch cubes. If the cheese has a rind on the outside, remove the rind first.

Distribute the cubes of cheese evenly in a small heatproof skillet or casserole dish.

Top with sliced garlic.

Drizzle on the olive oil.

Sprinkle with the Italian seasoning, salt, and pepper.

Place the pan under the broiler for 6 minutes or until the cheese is melted and bubbling and starts to brown. Check frequently.

Serve the baked cheese family-style right out of the oven in the pan with crusty chunks of bread for dipping.

Serves 8 as an appetizer

Southern Shrimp Butter

I didn't grow up eating Shrimp Butter in Nashville - we were a bit landlocked and great seafood wasn't as readily available as it is now. When I went to college I discovered this fantastic appetizer and don't know how I lived so long without it. Shrimp Butter is sort of like a seafood pate, delicious shrimp, just the right amount of spice, a judicious amount of sherry and, of course butter. You can serve it with crackers or on toast points made by baking bread cut into rectangles in a 250-degree oven for 30 minutes. It will most definitely be the hit at any party. Best of all, Shrimp Butter takes less than 15 minutes to put together, and you can make it ahead of time. Check out the bonus recipe if you're lucky enough to have leftovers.

INGREDIENTS

½ lb raw shrimp, peeled and deveined

1 stick butter

1 garlic clove, peeled

½ tsp each, salt and pepper (taste after blending – you can always add more)

1 tsp paprika

¼ cup sherry (you can use cooking sherry found with vinegars in the grocery store)

Juice of half of a lemon (about 1 tbsp)

Crackers or toast points for serving

DIRECTIONS

Melt 2 tbsp butter in a small skillet over medium high heat with the garlic clove.

When butter foams, add shrimp and sprinkle with salt, pepper and paprika.

Cook shrimp about 3 to 4 minutes turning once until pink and firm.

With a slotted spoon, remove shrimp and garlic from the skillet and put in a food processor.

Return skillet to heat, add sherry and lemon juice and cook for 1 minute.

Add sherry mixture to shrimp in the food processor and process for 1 minute.

Add butter to the food processor, one tbsp at a time, blending to combine after each addition. Continue to blend until smooth and silky, about 1 minute.

Cover and chill at least 2 hours or overnight.

Makes about 1½ cups.

Bonus Recipe: Shrimp Grits Casserole

Cook 4 servings of grits according to package directions. Preheat oven to 350 degrees. Stir ¼ cup (or more to taste) of shrimp butter into cooked grits. Spray an 8 x 8 casserole with cooking spray pour in grits mixture. Top with ¼ cup Parmesan cheese. Sprinkle with 1 tsp paprika. Bake for 20 minutes or until hot and lightly browned on top.

Fried Ravioli

Fried Ravioli is so simple to make and best of all, it's easy to keep the ingredients on hand. I love the variety of fillings for ravioli. They come stuffed with different cheeses, meats, seafood, and all sorts of vegetables. I once discovered pink heart-shaped ones for Valentine's Day. My current heartthrob is a spinach, sundried tomato, and ricotta combination, but I'm fickle and can fall for another any day. In fantasies where I'm a famous foodie, someone is interviewing me asking important questions, like what I stock in my freezer. Without mentioning the six or seven flavors of ice cream that take up the whole top shelf, I'll proudly announce that there are always several packages of ravioli tucked away in the freezer. That would be true, and is one of the reasons this became such a popular dish for my family. That and the fact that you can say, "Gee, I sure would like some Fried Ravioli," and be eating it in less than fifteen minutes

INGREDIENTS

1 pkg refrigerated ravioli, with any filling you like (a 20 oz package serves 4 hungry friends)

1 tbsp salt

4 tbsp canola oil

Parmesan cheese (the kind in a can is fine)

1 jar pizza or pasta sauce (the jar sizes differ by brand—you need about 1½ cups, so pick your favorite)

DIRECTIONS

Bring a large pot of water with one tbsp of salt to a boil and add the ravioli.

Boil for about 2 minutes and drain well. Pat dry with paper towels.

Heat oil in a large skillet over medium-high heat; add ravioli in batches of 12 to 15 at a time, and fry, turning to get both sides crispy. It only takes a couple of minutes for both sides to cook.

Drain on paper towels and sprinkle with Parmesan cheese.

Heat sauce in a bowl in the microwave, and serve on the side for dipping.

Serves 4

Fun Ways to Serve Popcorn

INGREDIENTS

First of all, **do not** buy over-priced, weirdly seasoned, smelly microwave popcorn.

Do buy a bag of plain popcorn, probably hidden on the bottom shelf at the grocery store below the microwave stuff.

I like white popcorn better than yellow. Keep it in a jar.

Buy brown paper lunch sacks, sold with Baggies and plastic wrap.

DIRECTIONS

Put 2 handfuls (about ⅓ cup) of popcorn in a brown-paper lunch bag and fold over the top.

Microwave for 1½ to 2 minutes—just listen for when the popping almost stops. Now you have popcorn.

Spray with butter-flavored cooking spray and add salt.

That's just basic popcorn. Here are more ideas:

- » Add pepper.
- » Drizzle with little maple syrup and add a pinch of cayenne pepper. Try maple syrup and cinnamon for kettle corn.
- » Add Parmesan cheese and Italian seasoning, taco seasoning, dry ranch-dressing mix, five-spice powder, or Montreal steak seasoning.
- » Add M&M'S *see note, and, if you want, raisins, mini pretzels, mini chocolate chips and/or mini marshmallows.
- » Add some of the seasoning packet from Ramen noodles, peanuts, and chow mein noodles.

*You can make this **seasonal** by using M&M'S which are available every year in special colors: orange and black for Halloween; red and green for Christmas; pink for Valentine's Day; pastels for Easter; and red, white, and blue for the Fourth of July. How cool is that!

Suggestion: Here's my little secret: I "re-pop" the kernels that don't pop the first time. Just put them back in the bag and pop. They taste even better! Crazy, huh?

Guacamole

I have a long- standing love affair with avocados. When I was growing up, they seemed completely exotic. My mother called them "avocado pears," and I just thought they were some strange fruit from the West Coast. Actually one of my favorite things to eat is avocado spread on toast. Is that weird? I like avocado soup, stuffed avocados, avocado in salads, avocado enchiladas…it's a long list.
Start with this— delicious!

INGREDIENTS

> 2 avocados, pitted and peeled (if they are really hard, they aren't ripe yet)
>
> Juice of 1 lime or 1 tbsp bottled lime juice
>
> 1 tsp salt
>
> ¼ tsp ground cumin
>
> ¼ cup diced onion (about ½ of a small onion)
>
> Optional: 3 tbsp fresh cilantro, chopped
>
> 1 pinch ground cayenne pepper or a dash of hot sauce

DIRECTIONS

> In a medium bowl, mash together the avocados with the lime juice, salt, and cumin.
>
> Mix in onion and cilantro, if using.
>
> Stir in cayenne pepper.
>
> Cover and refrigerate 1 hour, or eat immediately if you just can't wait.
>
> *Makes about 1½ cups*
>
> **Suggestion:** If you like tomatoes in your guacamole, dice one small Roma and add (grocery store salad bar).

Bonus Recipe: Pico de Gallo

In a food processor, combine 4 to 6 Roma tomatoes, quartered; ½ onion cut in 4 pieces; 1 small, seeded jalapeno pepper; 1 tbsp lime juice; 1 tbsp cilantro (optional); and ½ tsp salt. Pulse several times until coarsely chopped. Serve with chips.

Ham and Cheese Pizza Rolls

INGREDIENTS

4 tbsp olive oil

1 clove garlic, chopped (you can use the garlic in a jar)

1 tsp Italian seasoning or oregano

Flour, for work surface

1 roll refrigerated pizza dough (in canned biscuit section)

1 cup shredded cheddar cheese

⅓ lb sliced ham (honey ham from the store deli is excellent)

DIRECTIONS

Preheat oven to 350 degrees.

Spray a baking sheet with cooking spray. *(hint: Line baking sheet with aluminum foil before spraying for easy cleanup.)*

In a small bowl, mix the olive oil, garlic, and Italian seasoning.

On a lightly floured surface, roll out the pizza dough a bit to flatten. *(hint: Use wax paper on your counter and put a little flour on it.)*

Brush the entire surface with the seasoned olive oil, saving about 1 tbsp of oil mixture for brushing the top of the rolls before baking.

Top with shredded cheese and an even layer of ham.

Roll up like a jelly roll.

Slice into ½ inch spirals and place on a baking sheet.

Brush on extra olive oil.

Bake 20 to 30 minutes.

Makes about 16

Serving Suggestion: You can serve these alone or with pizza sauce, heated in a small bowl in the microwave, or with honey mustard.

Suggestion: Omit ham for a **vegetarian version**.

Hot Artichoke Dip

This dip has probably been around since biblical times, but for some reason, no one is ever tired of it. Could it be because it's delicious? I like the addition of garlic salt and sherry in my version, but you could probably put garlic salt and sherry in just about anything and make it better. One time I stuffed this dip in scooped out tomatoes, baked them at 350 degrees for about 30 minutes, and served them as a side dish. Stuffed tomatoes—brilliant!

INGREDIENTS

14 oz can artichoke hearts, drained

1 cup mayonnaise (the kind made with olive oil is healthier)

1 cup Parmesan cheese (the kind in the can is fine)

½ tsp garlic salt

Optional: 2 tbsp sherry (you can use cooking sherry found with vinegars in the grocery store)

DIRECTIONS

Preheat the oven to 350 degrees.

Chop up artichoke hearts a little.

Mix with cheese, mayonnaise, garlic salt, and sherry, if using.

Put in a small baking dish and bake for 30 minutes.

Serve with crackers or bagel chips or even carrot chips.

Makes about 2 cups

Bonus Recipe: Hot Spinach Artichoke Dip

Follow the same basic recipe with the following changes: use only ½ cup mayonnaise and add 6 oz of cream cheese.

Add 1 cup of chopped, frozen spinach, thawed.

Mix and bake as directed in the original recipe.

That's it!

Hot Baby Reubens

These Reubens are a great little treat for entertaining because you can put everything together the day before, cover with foil, and put in the fridge overnight. Just pop the Reubens in the oven when you're ready. Recipes like this make entertaining a breeze.

INGREDIENTS

2 pkg dinner rolls *(hint: The frozen ones in aluminum pans make this super easy.)*

¾ lb thinly sliced deli pastrami, beef or turkey

½ lb sliced Swiss cheese

1 bottle Thousand Island dressing (or make you own, page 26)

Sauerkraut (with canned vegetables at the grocery store)

DIRECTIONS

Preheat the oven to 325 degrees.

Remove rolls from packages. Cut rolls in half. *(hint: If they are still a little frozen, it's easy to cut the whole thing instead of individual rolls.)*

Spread dressing on cut sides of the top and bottom of each roll.

To the bottom half, layer cheese, pastrami, and sauerkraut and put tops back on.

Cover with foil.

Bake for 20 to 25 minutes or until cheese is melted.

Slice into individual sandwiches.

Makes 32 sandwiches

Suggestion: Change it up: omit the sauerkraut, experiment with different cheeses, and try with roast beef; add mayo mixed with apricot preserves or marmalade; or use ham or turkey with honey mustard.

Meatball Sliders

This recipe calls for frozen meatballs, but you could definitely make your own by mixing ground beef or turkey with breadcrumbs, a beaten egg, Parmesan cheese, and Italian seasoning.(See Bonus Recipe) However, prepared meatballs are so easy to use and sometimes we all need a little short cut. These are fun to serve and a little different from the usual slider.

INGREDIENTS

1 pkg meatballs, turkey or beef (in frozen foods or with prepackaged deli meats; packages range in size from 16 to 24 oz) or make your own – Bonus Recipe

1 tbsp olive oil

1 jar pasta sauce (the jar sizes differ by brand—you need about 2 cups, so pick your favorite)

For serving: 1 pkg sliced mozzarella cheese

Optional: sautéed peppers and onions (grocery-store salad bar)

Bread of choice: I love those little Hawaiian bread rolls, but dinner rolls work too.

DIRECTIONS

Fry meatballs in oil in a large skillet over medium-high heat to brown.

Add sauce and let the meatballs simmer about 20 minutes.

Everyone can make their own sliders to taste.

Servings vary—count on 2 or 3 meatballs per person

Serving Suggestion: You could also put meatballs and sauce in your Crock-Pot on High for 1½ to 2 hours. It's great to serve that way for a party. Perfect for football game day!

Bonus Recipe: Meatballs

Mix 1 lb. lean ground turkey or beef with ½ cup dry breadcrumbs ½ cup Parmesan cheese, 1 beaten egg, 1 tsp salt, ¼ tsp red pepper flakes, and 2 tsp Italian seasoning or a mix of basil and oregano. Roll into individual meatballs about the size of a ping pong ball. Coat a large skillet with 1 tbsp olive or canola oil and fry meatballs over medium high heat until browned. Meatballs can also be baked in a baking dish sprayed with cooking spray for 20 minutes in a 400 degree oven. (Can be made ahead and frozen.)

Mini Calzones

INGREDIENTS

14 oz jar pizza sauce

1 cup grated mozzarella cheese

1 pkg pepperoni, turkey or regular, slightly chopped (mini pepperonis work well too)

1 pkg (2 crusts) roll-out piecrusts (find in the grocery store with canned biscuits and cookie dough, or make your own, page 63.)

1 egg, beaten, for egg wash *see note

½ cup grated Parmesan (the kind in the can works fine)

DIRECTIONS

Preheat oven to 350 degrees.

Spray 2 baking sheets with cooking spray. *(hint: Line baking sheet with aluminum foil before spraying for easy cleanup.)*

Stir the mozzarella cheese and pepperoni into pizza sauce.

Cut pie dough into large circles using a cup or a large biscuit cutter. *(hint: The plastic cups you get at sports events are a good size.)*

Place a spoonful of the sauce mixture in the middle of one half of the circle.

Fold the dough in half over the sauce mixture. Press edges with tines of a fork to seal. Place on prepared baking sheets.

Brush with egg wash* and generously sprinkle with Parmesan cheese.

Bake until golden, about 15 to 20 minutes.

Remove from oven and sprinkle with a little Parmesan cheese.

Makes 12 to 14 depending on size of dough circles

*To make an egg wash you just beat up eggs with a fork and brush the mixture on the pastry. If that seems like too much trouble or you don't have eggs, or both, spray with a little cooking spray. You can use a small clean (new!) paintbrush as a pastry brush.

Suggestion: The leftover pizza dough does not roll out well, but you can twist it into small breadsticks and bake it along with the calzones. Heat leftover sauce mixture in the microwave, and serve it as a dipping sauce with the breadsticks. There's no waste, plus you get two appetizers for the price of one! Omit pepperoni for a **vegetarian version**.

Spinach Balls

This is a very un-glamorous name for something so tasty. I tried to think of another title for this recipe, but I couldn't, because that's what they are. Make them regardless of the name. They are spectacular and even my spinach-hating friends (and son) love this appetizer. Pop extras in a Baggie to reheat later. Or eat them cold standing in front of your fridge around 2:00 a.m. like I do.

INGREDIENTS

2 (10 oz) pkg. frozen, chopped spinach

2 cups herb-seasoned stuffing mix (in the baking section at the grocery store)

1 cup grated Parmesan cheese (the kind in the can is fine)

4 eggs

1½ sticks melted butter

2 tsp pepper, add more for extra heat

¼ cup onion, chopped (about half of a small one)

¼ tsp nutmeg

DIRECTIONS

Preheat oven to 350 degrees.

Cook spinach according to microwave directions on the package.

Put spinach in a colander to drain.

When it cools enough to handle, squeeze it as dry as you can with your hands.

In a large bowl combine all ingredients.

Shape into round balls a little smaller than a ping-pong ball.

Put on a baking sheet. *(hint: Line baking sheet with aluminum foil for easy cleanup.)*

Bake for about 15 to 20 minutes until firm.

Makes about 35 to 40 spinach balls

Suggestion: You could easily cut this recipe in half, or you can make it all and freeze half of the spinach balls, uncooked, on a baking sheet until firm. Store them in a Baggie in the freezer.

Sweet Hot Chicken and Bacon Bites

Wow! The first time I made these Sweet Hot Chicken and Bacon Bites they disappeared before I had a chance to taste one. Everyone loves chicken and bacon. The next time Sweet Hot Chicken and Bacon Bites were on the menu, I grabbed one before I served them. Make sure you do that too!

INGREDIENTS

1 to 1½ lb boneless, skinless, chicken breasts

12 to 16 oz pkg sliced bacon

⅔ cup brown sugar

2 tbsp chili powder

1 tsp garlic salt

Wooden toothpicks (baking section at grocery store)

DIRECTIONS

Preheat oven to 350 degrees.

Spray a baking sheet with cooking spray. *(hint: Line baking sheet with aluminum foil before spraying for easy cleanup.)*

Cut chicken breasts into 1-inch cubes. (Rinse chicken first—remember clean work surface and clean hands.)

Cut each bacon slice into thirds. *(hint: I keep a pair of regular scissors in the kitchen just for cutting up food. They're great for snipping fresh herbs too. Scissors go in the dishwasher.)*

Wrap each chicken cube with bacon and secure with a toothpick.

Stir together brown sugar, chili powder, and garlic salt.

Dredge bacon-wrapped chicken in brown sugar mixture.

Place chicken on prepared pan and bake for 30 to 35 minutes or until bacon is crisp. Pour off any accumulated bacon grease halfway through cooking.

Serves 8 to 10 as an appetizer

Suggestion: Put these on skewers for a dinner. Add vegetables to your skewers—like green or red pepper, onions, mushrooms, and cherry tomatoes (grocery store salad bar)— and you have a delicious dinner. A little rice or a baked potato would take it up to sublime! Be sure to turn the skewers over about halfway through cooking for even browning.

INTRODUCTION TO
Soups and Salads

Even though soup and salad get a separate listing from entrées, either one can stand alone as a meal. My Favorite Italian Soup is a five-minute undertaking, and if served with some crusty French or Italian bread, and maybe a dish of sorbet for dessert, would impress the pickiest eater. Plus, the price is right on that one! The French Onion Soup makes a very elegant meal with toasted bread and melting cheese on the top. Creamy Chicken Noodle Soup is everyone's favorite comfort food. Remember that soup can be an easy and inexpensive way to entertain friends. Black Bean Soup is one of my favorite recipes to make for company. It's warm, comforting, and just a little bit exotic. There are several additional soups listed in the Crock-Pot/ Slow Cooker section as well.

Any salad with a little protein of your choice added is a perfect light supper. I like to mix a can of drained tuna with a can of garbanzo beans plus whatever looks good on the grocery store salad bar, and dress with a little olive oil and a squeeze of lemon for the easiest meal ever. Do not forget leftovers to use in both salads and soups. That extra piece of chicken or salmon from last night's dinner can top a salad of romaine lettuce with Caesar Dressing, recipe page 37, and be a gourmet experience. Leftover chicken can also help you make a satisfying and simple chicken noodle soup for one with some pasta and a couple of chicken bouillon cubes. Leftover steak just cries out to be paired with the Tomato Dressing and Steak Sauce, recipe page 59. Don't forget there are recipes for simple salad dressings beginning on page 39 that can dress up any salad to perfection.

Of course soup or salad can be a very lovely start to any meal. Just keep an open mind, go ahead, and play around with these basic recipes. Remember, you are your own chef!

A Few Basic Salad Dressings

Fresh salad dressing always trumps the store- bought varieties. You control the oil and salt and make sure ingredients are fresh. These are all easy to prepare. The directions are the same for all: put the ingredients in a jar, **and shake them up.** The dressing should keep at least a week in the refrigerator. Try different vinegars for different tastes, and experiment with fresh herbs. Once you get hooked on these dressings, you'll forget you ever bought those bottles from the store.

Good salad greens: romaine lettuce, spinach, endive, iceberg lettuce, fresh herbs

Good salad toppings: toasted nuts, berries, bean sprouts, dried fruit, hard-boiled eggs, beans, sliced veggies including onions, peppers, mushrooms, cucumbers, tomatoes, beets, carrots—add protein like leftover chicken, salmon, shrimp, or steak and it's a meal!

BLUE CHEESE DRESSING

½ cup mayonnaise (the kind made with olive oil is healthier)

¼ cup sour cream

1 clove garlic, chopped

1 tbsp lemon juice or vinegar

½ tsp sugar

1 tsp salt

2 drops of hot sauce (more to taste)

½ cup blue cheese, crumbled

Makes about 1 cup

CAESAR DRESSING (WITHOUT RAW EGG)

¾ cup mayonnaise (the kind made with olive oil is healthier)

2 anchovy filets, mashed, or 1 tsp anchovy paste (you can find this with canned tuna and other canned fish in the grocery store)

1tbsp lemon juice

1 tsp Worcestershire sauce

1 clove garlic, chopped

½ cup Parmesan cheese, grated

½ tsp each, salt and pepper

Optional: add milk a tablespoon at a time if you want a thinner dressing

Makes about 1 cup

ITALIAN DRESSING

6 tbsp olive oil

2 tbsp red or white wine vinegar

1 tbsp lemon juice

1 garlic clove, chopped

1 tsp dried basil

¼ tsp red pepper flakes

¼ tsp dried oregano

1 tsp salt

Makes about ½ cup

RASPBERRY VINAIGRETTE

½ cup frozen raspberries, thawed

¼ cup olive oil

¼ cup honey

2 tbsp lemon juice

⅛ tsp salt

Combine all ingredients in the blender for a smoother dressing.

Makes about 1 cup

SESAME DRESSING

½ cup rice vinegar

2 tbsp mirin (Japanese sweet cooking wine, found in the Asian foods section of the grocery store – substitute sherry if you can't find mirin)

2 tbsp canola oil

2 tsp sesame oil

3 tbsp sugar

2 tbsp soy sauce

¼ tsp salt

1 tbsp sesame seeds

Makes about ¾ cup

THOUSAND ISLAND OR RUSSIAN DRESSING (GREAT ON BURGERS TOO!)

½ cup mayonnaise (the kind made with olive oil is healthier)

2 tbsp ketchup

2 tbsp pickle relish

2 tbsp lemon juice

1 tsp Worcestershire sauce

¼ tsp salt

Makes about ¾ cup

SALAD FOR ONE: A SIMPLE DRESSING

¼ cup olive oil

2 tbsp of vinegar (any kind) or lemon juice

Pinch of salt and pepper

Asian Salad

It's a myth that only starving college students eat Ramen noodles. Ramen noodles can dress up a salad, take a starring role in a stir-fry, or serve as a satisfying lunch for a busy person who keeps a package or two around for an emergency. You will adore the crunch in this salad!

INGREDIENTS

⅔ cup vegetable oil, plus 1 tsp for sautéing

1 pkg Ramen noodles, any flavor

¼ cup sliced almonds

⅓ cup sugar

⅓ cup vinegar

1 pkg fresh spinach

¼ cup each: green onions and shredded carrots (grocery store salad bar)

1 small can drained mandarin oranges

Optional: bean sprouts

DIRECTIONS

Add 1 tsp oil to a small skillet over medium heat.

Break up Ramen noodles and sauté with the almonds until lightly browned. Set aside.

Place oil, sugar, vinegar, and seasoning packet from the noodles in a jar.

Shake well to combine.

Put spinach in a salad bowl with green onions, carrots, mandarin oranges, and bean sprouts, if using.

Top with noodles and nuts.

Dress with as much dressing as needed and reserve the rest for another salad.

Toss. (*hint: Don't add dressing until you are ready to serve.*)

Serves 4 to 6

Black Bean Soup

Once I had Black Bean Soup at a restaurant in Phoenix, and the waiter brought the soup to the table along with a dainty little pitcher of sherry. I have this thing about sherry, and I thought it was the most wonderful presentation ever. So yes, even if I'm eating Black Bean Soup all alone, I pour sherry into my little sherry pitcher. You should do that. It makes you feel special every time.

INGREDIENTS

2 tbsp olive oil

1 onion, chopped

1 carrot, chopped

4 garlic cloves, chopped

2 tsp cumin

1 tsp oregano

1 tsp chopped jalapeño (you can use the pickled ones in a jar)

2 cans black beans, undrained

1 can diced tomatoes, undrained

1½ cups chicken broth

½ tsp salt (taste because the salt varies in chicken broth by brand)

¼ tsp pepper

Pepper to taste

Optional garnishes: sherry, diced green onion, grated cheese, cubed avocado, lime juice, cilantro, and sour cream

DIRECTIONS

Heat oil in heavy large pot over medium-high heat.

Add onion, carrot, and garlic; sauté until vegetables begin to soften, about 6 minutes.

Stir in cumin, oregano, and jalapeño.

Add beans, tomatoes with juice, and broth; bring soup to boil.

Reduce heat to simmer, cover, and cook until carrots are tender, about 15 minutes.

Transfer 3 cups of soup to blender and puree until smooth. (*hint: Put a dish towel over the blender before you turn it on in case any hot liquid escapes.*)

Return puree to pot.

Simmer soup until slightly thickened, about 15 minutes.

Season to taste with salt and pepper.

Serves 4

Broccoli Salad

This is the recipe that convinced my son to eat broccoli. Take Broccoli Salad to a picnic or potluck, and it will be the first thing to disappear. Leftovers are great the next day.

INGREDIENTS

1 cup mayonnaise (the kind made with olive oil is healthier)

½ cup sugar

2 tbsp vinegar

1 head broccoli, washed and separated into florets including stems, and chopped into bite size pieces

½ cup raisins or dried cranberries *see note for this and next 3 ingredients

¼ cup onion, chopped*

½ cup sunflower seeds*

¼ cup bacon bits*

DIRECTIONS

In a small bowl, mix together the mayonnaise, sugar, and vinegar.

In a large salad bowl combine the remaining ingredients except bacon.

Add the dressing and toss well to coat.

Refrigerate for an hour or until ready to serve.

Top with the bacon bits.

Serves 6

*To make this really easy, get raisins, onion, sunflower seeds, and bacon at the salad bar. Pack bacon in a separate container.

Caprese Salad

I have a friend who will order this salad anywhere it's on the menu, any time of year. It should be named for her. I'm a little more of a tomato snob and love a summer vine- ripened tomato, but in the winter a Roma tomato is a fair substitute when she's coming to dinner. It's a beautiful presentation and so simple to prepare.

INGREDIENTS *See Note

1 tomato per person

Fresh mozzarella cheese, (usually sold in plastic containers in the cheese section at the grocery store, not the sliced cheese in the deli) enough to have 3 slices about the diameter of the tomato slices per serving

Fresh basil, 3 or 4 leaves per serving

Olive oil to drizzle

Salt and pepper

DIRECTIONS

Slice tomato into thick slices, about 4 per tomato.

Layer tomato slices with slices of cheese and fresh basil on individual serving plates. *(hint: You could do this on a large platter for a crowd. It makes a very pretty presentation.)*

Drizzle with about a tbsp of olive oil per serving and sprinkle with salt and pepper.

*This is a salad where the ingredient amounts are based on the number of people you are serving. The amounts listed are for one person; just keep adding for more people.

Suggestion: At the local markets in the summer, you can find all kinds of heirloom tomatoes in different colors. Those make a beautiful salad. Fresh ground pepper makes a difference! The salad looks elegant, but it's really simple.

Creamy Chicken Noodle Soup

INGREDIENTS

3 tbsp butter

1 cup each, chopped onions, sliced celery, shredded carrots (grocery store salad bar)

3 tbsp flour

6 cups chicken broth

1 cup half & half or whole milk

1 lb boneless, skinless, chicken breasts, cut in bite-size pieces *see note (Rinse chicken first—remember clean work surface and clean hands.)

1 cup dry penne pasta (you could substitute another pasta), cooked according to package directions

Optional: ¼ cup snap peas, sliced or green peas

3 tbsp lemon juice

Salt (Chicken broth varies in salt content by brand so you really need to taste the soup.)

¼ tsp pepper

DIRECTIONS

Melt butter in a large heavy pot over medium heat.

Add vegetables and cook until tender, about 5 minutes.

Add flour to vegetables and cook 1 minute stirring constantly.

Stir in chicken broth.

Bring to a low simmer and add half & half or milk, simmer 5 minutes, and add chicken.

Simmer another 5 minutes until chicken is done.

Mix in cooked pasta, snap or green peas, if using, and simmer 2 more minutes.

Stir in lemon juice and season to taste with salt and pepper.

Serves 4

*You could use rotisserie chicken or leftover chicken

French Onion Soup

French Onion Soup manages to be classic comfort food and sophisticated at the same time. Don't think you can only have this as restaurant fare. It is infinitely better homemade and hot from your very own kitchen. I always have French Onion Soup with a salad of romaine or endive lettuce and blue cheese dressing, see **Bonus Recipe**, because once I went to a restaurant in New York where the waiter insisted I have this salad with my onion soup. I loved it.

INGREDIENTS

½ stick butter

2 lb onions, about 3 large, peeled, halved lengthwise, then thinly sliced

½ tsp thyme

1 bay leaf

½ tsp each salt, pepper, and sugar

1 tbsp flour

¾ cup white wine (you can use cooking wine found with vinegars in the grocery store) *see note for substitution

5 cups beef broth (you can use bouillon cubes)

Sliced French bread

Sliced Swiss cheese

DIRECTIONS

Melt butter in a heavy pot over low heat.

Add onions, thyme, bay leaf, salt, pepper, and sugar and cook, stirring occasionally, until onions are soft and golden brown, about 45 minutes.

Add flour and cook, stirring, 1 minute.

Raise heat to medium, add in wine and cook, stirring 1 minute.

Stir in broth and simmer, uncovered, stirring occasionally for 30 minutes.

After soup has simmered for 15 minutes, preheat oven to 350 degrees.

Arrange bread on a large baking sheet *(hint: Line baking sheet with aluminum foil for easy cleanup.)* and toast, turning over once.

Remove bay leaf from the soup.

Taste for salt because salt content will vary depending on the broth you use.

Turn oven to broil.

Ladle soup into ovenproof bowls.

Top soup with toast, and top toast with Swiss cheese.

Broil 4 to 5 inches from heat until cheese is melted and bubbly, 1 to 2 minutes. *(hint: If your bowls aren't ovenproof, toast bread with cheese under the broiler and add to soup in the bowl.)*

Serves 4

*You can use apple juice or cider as a substitution. It has a bit of a sweeter taste.

Bonus Recipe: Romaine and Blue Cheese Salad with Candied Walnuts

Heat a small skillet over medium-high heat, and melt 2 tbsp of butter. Add ½ cup of walnuts and stir to coat with butter. Add 2 tbsp of sugar and ½ tsp of salt or garlic salt and a tiny pinch of cayenne pepper. Cook stirring until sugar melts and walnuts are browned, about 2 minutes. Pour on aluminum foil to cool. Break sugar coated nuts into small pieces and serve on top of chopped romaine lettuce dressed with blue cheese dressing, page 37.

Hot Nut Salad

This salad was originally an invention to deal with an overly zealous crop of basil, and it quickly became our "house salad." No one can resist this, when they smell the divine scent of almonds and garlic toasting in olive oil. The spinach and basil get slightly warm from the hot oil, the almonds and garlic are crunchy, and the Parmesan cheese is salty. This salad goes with everything. Make this for your next party or just have a big bowl of it all by yourself. Good either way.

INGREDIENTS

1 bag of baby spinach

1 bunch fresh basil (in produce section of the grocery store, sometimes in a plastic box)

4 tbsp olive oil

4 cloves garlic, peeled and sliced

⅓ cup sliced almonds

¼ cup grated Parmesan cheese (the dry kind in the can works best)

Salt and pepper to taste, depending on the size of your salad

DIRECTIONS

Put the spinach and basil leaves in a large salad bowl and toss.

Heat olive oil in small skillet.

Add garlic and almonds and sauté until lightly browned.

Pour hot oil, garlic, and almonds over salad, stirring to distribute.

Add salt, pepper, and Parmesan and give a final stir.

Serves 4

Serving Suggestion: To make this salad for company, put the spinach and basil in a large salad bowl. Add salt and pepper and set aside. Put oil in a small skillet and add almonds and sliced garlic. It can all sit at room temperature for a couple of hours until you're ready to cook the almonds and garlic and serve the salad.

Julia Child's Potato Salad—Rewritten for Mortals

INGREDIENTS

2 lb Yukon Gold potatoes or red potatoes

1 tbsp salt for water to boil potatoes

2 tbsp vinegar

½ cup each, chopped onion and celery (grocery-store salad bar)

3 tbsp chopped sweet pickle or pickle relish

1 tsp each, salt and pepper

1 cup mayonnaise (the kind made with olive oil is healthier)

DIRECTIONS

You don't have to peel the potatoes, just cut into cubes about ½ inch each.

Put the potatoes in a pan with cold water to cover.

Heat to a simmer, add 1 tbsp salt, and cook the potatoes for 8 to 10 minutes, until just cooked through. Bite into a cube to be sure.

Immediately remove from the heat and drain the potatoes, saving a ⅓ cup of the cooking liquid for dressing.

Put potatoes in a bowl.

Stir the cider vinegar and ⅓ cup of the cooking liquid together in a small bowl, and pour over the potato pieces.

Let sit 10 minutes to absorb the liquid.

Add the onion, celery, pickle, salt and pepper, and mayonnaise and fold everything together until well blended.

Taste and add more salt, pepper, or mayonnaise as needed.

Cover the salad and set aside in the refrigerator for at least an hour before serving.

Serves 8 to 10

OPTIONAL GARNISHES (grocery store salad bar)

3 or 4 slices crisply cooked bacon, crumbled

2 chopped hard-boiled eggs

2 tbsp green onions

4 radishes, chopped

My Favorite Italian Soup

This soup is the perfect dinner for one but easy to make for more people. My son actually triples the amount of garlic. He makes this all the time for a late-night treat and swears it will cure a cold. This recipe takes less than 10 minutes to prepare from beginning to bowl!

INGREDIENTS

1 tbsp butter

1 tbsp olive oil

2 cloves garlic, chopped (use fresh, not from a jar)

2 tbsp flour

2 cups chicken broth (you can use bouillon cubes)

2 eggs

¼ cup grated Parmesan cheese

Salt and pepper to taste (salt content varies by brand in chicken broth, so you do need to taste)

DIRECTIONS

In a medium-sized pot, melt butter with olive oil.

Add garlic and cook for 2 minutes, stirring frequently.

Add flour and cook, stirring constantly, for 1 minute.

Whisk in chicken broth (*hint: Heat it in the microwave to make it easier to combine with the flour.*)

Bring to a boil.

Beat eggs and Parmesan together in a small bowl.

Add the egg mixture slowly to the boiling soup, stirring constantly so the egg mixture forms little noodles.

Season to taste with salt and pepper.

Serves 1 for dinner or 2 as a first course

Serving Suggestion: Serve with crusty French or Italian bread.

Pasta Salad

INGREDIENTS

20 oz pkg cheese tortellini

1 cup Caesar or ranch salad dressing

¼ cup Parmesan cheese, grated (fresh is best, canned is OK)

salt and pepper (different dressings have different salt contents, so you do need to taste)

Pick ¼ to ½ of a cup each of three or four of these ingredients - add more ingredients if you feel adventurous! *(hint: Lots of these ingredients are available at the grocery store salad bar or deli.)*

Green or red onions; carrots; radishes; cherry tomatoes; sundried tomatoes; broccoli; red, yellow, or green peppers; zucchini or yellow squash; artichoke hearts; asparagus; peas; olives; three-bean salad; garbanzo beans; capers; pepperoncini; chopped pepperoni; cooked shrimp; cooked, cubed chicken; cooked, diced ham; cooked, sliced steak.

DIRECTIONS

Cook pasta according to package directions.

Drain and mix with dressing and cheese.

Add more dressing or cheese as needed.

Mix with selected items.

Serves 6

Popcorn Soup

A very clever presentation…

INGREDIENTS

3 ears of fresh corn or 1½ cups frozen corn

2 cups milk

1 onion, chopped

2 tbsp butter

2 tbsp flour

2 cups half & half or whole milk

½ tsp each, salt and pepper

Fresh popped buttered popcorn *see note

DIRECTIONS

Cut corn from cob if you're using fresh corn.

Put corn kernels and milk in a large saucepan and bring to a boil.

Reduce heat and simmer for 5 minutes.

Remove from heat.

Sauté onions in butter until soft, about 5 minutes.

Stir in flour and cook for 1 minute.

Add half & half, stirring constantly.

Add corn in milk, and salt and pepper.

Cook until thick, about 10 minutes.

Garnish with popcorn.

Serves 4

*See page 22 for the best way to make popcorn.

Spicy Noodle, Green Bean, and Carrot Salad

INGREDIENTS

DRESSING

¼ cup lime juice

3 tbsp vegetable oil

3 tbsp soy sauce

2 tbsp brown sugar

1 tbsp sesame oil

1 clove garlic, chopped (you can use garlic in the jar)

⅛ tsp red pepper flakes or to taste

1 tbsp sesame seeds

SALAD

½ lb green beans, cut diagonally into ½-inch pieces (snap off any stems first)

1 tbsp salt for water to cook beans and pasta

8 oz linguine or angel-hair pasta

1 cup each, shredded carrots, sliced green onions (grocery store salad bar)

DIRECTIONS

Put all ingredients for the dressing in a jar and shake them up.

Cook green beans in large pot of boiling salted water until crisp-tender, 3 to 4 minutes.

Using a slotted spoon, transfer beans to cold water to cool, leaving boiling water for pasta.

Drain when beans are cool.

Add pasta to boiling water and cook until just tender.

Drain pasta and rinse under cold water to cool to room temperature.

Combine green beans, pasta, carrots, green onions, and dressing in large bowl.

Toss to coat.

Serves 4

Suggestion: The dressing in the recipe is just wonderful. Why not make extra for a salad later in the week? It would be good on a spinach salad. Add strawberries and almonds for something really special.

Simple Wilted Kale Salad

We make this salad frequently and always called it Massaged Kale Salad, but Richard thought that sounded too weird so it's had a renaming. You really do work it with your hands to get a great texture, but don't let that stop you - it's fun to play with food. Call it "hand tossed". Plus, this salad is not only unique and delicious dish, but it's also very good for you. Kale is available all the time, so keep this on your list of favorite salads.

INGREDIENTS

1 small bunch of kale, stems removed, leaves thinly sliced

juice of 1 lemon

¼ cup olive oil

2 tbsp honey

salt and pepper to taste

¼ cup dried cranberries

¼ cup sunflower seeds – you could probably use any nut or even pumpkin seeds

DIRECTIONS

In a large bowl mix lemon juice, olive oil and honey.

Add kale and mix it with your hands for a minute or two until it starts to soften.

Add salt and pepper and taste.

Add dried cranberries and sunflower seeds and toss to combine.

This should serve 4 to 6 people depending on how much kale was in your bunch!

Suggestion: This is a gorgeous salad to serve during the Thanksgiving and Christmas seasons. Pomegranates are all over the grocery that time of year so you can substitute pomegranate seeds for the dried cranberries for a special touch.

Serving Suggestion: This can be made several hours ahead of time and refrigerated until serving time.

Spinach Salad with Hot Bacon Dressing

INGREDIENTS

4 slices of bacon

1 bag of spinach

½ onion, sliced thinly

½ tsp each, salt and pepper

2 tbsp sugar

2 tbsp vinegar

2 sliced hard-boiled eggs *see note

DIRECTIONS

Put spinach in a large salad bowl and the onion slices on top.

Sprinkle with salt and pepper.

Cook bacon in a skillet large enough not to crowd it, over medium-high heat.

Remove cooked bacon to a paper towel to drain, cool slightly and crumble into small pieces

Remove all but 2 tbsp of fat from skillet.

Add sugar to skillet to dissolve and add vinegar (the mixture steams when the vinegar goes in).

Stir to combine and immediately pour over spinach. Toss.

Top with bacon and eggs.

Serves 4

*To make a perfect hard-boiled egg put as many eggs as you need in a saucepan. Cover with cold water. Add a pinch of salt to make the eggs easier to peel. Bring the water to boil and allow it to boil for one full minute. Cover pan and remove from heat for 15 minutes. Drain eggs and run under cold water to cool.

Tomato Dressing and Steak Sauce

This dressing is so delicious on vine-ripened summer tomatoes and thinly sliced Vidalia onions. If it's the dead of winter and you want this anyway, use Roma or plum tomatoes. It's also tasty with grilled steak. The dressing keeps in the fridge for about 2 weeks.

INGREDIENTS

¼ cup red wine vinegar

4 tbsp brown sugar

1 tbsp Worcestershire sauce

8 oz can tomato sauce

2 tbsp olive oil

1 tsp salt

DIRECTIONS

In a small saucepan over medium heat, combine vinegar, sugar, Worcestershire sauce, and salt.

Allow sugar to dissolve in vinegar and liquids to come to a bubble.

Remove the saucepan from the heat and whisk in tomato sauce, then olive oil.

Let dressing cool and refrigerate.

Makes about 1½ cups

TO SERVE AS A SALAD:

3 beefsteak tomatoes, sliced ½-inch thick

1 Vidalia onion, thinly sliced

Arrange sliced tomatoes and onions on a serving platter.

Season tomatoes and onions with salt and pepper, to taste.

Pour dressing over the tomatoes and onions.

Serves 3

Taco Soup

This is a favorite for a crowd, plus any leftovers freeze well and can be a lifesaver on a busy day. The ounces for each can aren't listed because they vary slightly by brands. I would hate for anyone to skip making this recipe because of an ounce!

INGREDIENTS

1 lb ground beef or turkey

1 can pinto beans

1 can whole-kernel corn

1 can green beans

1 can ranch beans, undrained

1 can stewed tomatoes

2 cups beef broth (you can use bouillon cubes)

1 can diced tomatoes and green chiles (get mild unless you really like heat)

1 pkg taco seasoning mix

1 pkg ranch dressing mix (find this dry mix with bottled dressing at the grocery store)

Corn tortilla chips

DIRECTIONS

Brown meat in a large pot or Dutch oven, stirring until it crumbles and is no longer pink. *(hint: Remember that meat won't brown if there is liquid in the pan from the meat. Remove liquid with a spoon.)*

Rinse and drain pinto beans, corn, and green beans and add to pot.

Add remaining ingredients except tortilla chips.

Reduce heat; simmer 30 minute.

Ladle soup into bowls, and top with tortilla chips.

Serves 6

Serving Suggestion: You can offer garnishes: cheese, green onions, cilantro, and sliced black olives if you like.

Entrées

It's called the main dish for a reason—the entrée is the star of the show. When I plan a meal, whether it's just for family or for a group of friends, the entrée is always the first thing I pick. After that it's okay to play around with side dishes and dessert ideas. The entrées in this section were selected not only because they are all delicious, but also because they are recipes you will always enjoy preparing and eating while feeling confident that the dish will be perfect every time.

A family favorite is Asian Beef and Noodles, page 67, which comes together quickly with the help of prewashed, bagged produce, and your grocery store salad bar. I've never met anyone who doesn't adore Taco Pizza, page 95. The only hard part of that recipe is to remember to thaw the dough. Fish in Foil, page 81, is healthy and easy—difficult to beat that combo. New Orleans Barbeque Shrimp, page 89, is great for a party, and since no one would believe it took you ten minutes to assemble, don't tell them! Many of these entrées need only a salad or a loaf of bread to be a complete meal. I would be remiss not to mention that several other chapters have main-dish ideas as well. We love breakfast for dinner and a good soup on a rainy night is hard to beat!

The recipes will be your classics you'll make and enjoy time and again.

This chapter has a lot of shopping tips and hints. There are ideas for serving and entertaining as well. So get busy and make yourself a delicious dinner. You may even want to share with a friend, but he or she better deserve it, because it will be a treat!

How to Cook Chicken for a Casserole

There are several easy ways to get 2½ to 3 cups of cooked, chopped chicken breasts. Pick what works best for you.

1. **Poaching**: You will need a 1 to 1½ lb package of skinless, boneless, uncooked chicken breasts, or a 3 lb package of whole, uncooked, chicken breasts. Rinse breasts in cold water. Place chicken in a large saucepan and just cover with water and 2 tsp salt. Bring water to a boil then reduce heat to a simmer. Simmer for 10 minutes, and remove pan from heat. Let chicken cool in broth for 20 minutes before you chop it. Add 10 minutes of cooking time if you are using whole chicken breasts. Remove skin and bones before chopping.

2. **Sautéing**: You will need a 1 to 1½ lb package of skinless, boneless, uncooked chicken breasts. Rinse breasts in cold water, and pat dry. Heat 1 tbsp of olive or canola oil over medium-high heat in a large skillet. Lightly salt and pepper both sides of the chicken breasts. Sauté chicken in the skillet for 2½ minutes on the first side. Turn over and sauté 1 minute on the second side. Add ¼ cup of liquid—chicken broth, wine, sherry, or water to the skillet. Cover with a tight-fitting lid. Remove from heat and let rest 10 minutes. Uncover and cool for 10 more minutes before chopping.

3. You can also use a rotisserie chicken. Remove skin and remove meat from bones. Chop.

Substitution Recipe for Canned Soup

Canned soup is definitely a convenience food, and there is nothing wrong with tossing it in a casserole or Crock-Pot. That being said, if you want only the freshest taste and object to using canned soup or don't have any in the pantry, this is a the recipe for a homemade replacement.

Melt 5 tbsp of butter in a medium saucepan over medium heat. Sauté ¼ cup of the ingredient in your soup (such as mushrooms or celery) until softened. For cream of chicken, add a little chicken bouillon. Stir in 5 tbsp of flour and whisk for 1 minute. Add 2 cups milk and stir until thick. Add ½ tsp salt or to taste.

Replaces 1 can of soup.

How to Make a Piecrust

You can buy a piecrust at the grocery, but a piecrust is easy to make, particularly if you have a food processor. It only involves four ingredients, one being water! If you don't have a food processor, mix by hand. It's still easy. Give it a try.

You will need 1¼ cups flour, ½ tsp salt, 1 stick of butter, and ¼ cup cold water.

Put the butter in the freezer for 10 minutes. Remove and cut into tablespoon size pieces. Put 1¼ cups of flour and ½ tsp salt in the food processor and give it 3 or 4 quick pulses to combine. Add butter and give it 5 or 6 quick pulses to form a crumbly mixture. Add the water about 1 tbsp at a time, pulsing after each addition. Stop adding water when the ingredients come together. Remove mixture from processor and form in a ball. Wrap in plastic wrap or put in a large Baggie and flatten to a disk. Refrigerate for an hour before using.

Bonus Recipe: Five-Minute Alfredo Sauce

Melt 2 tbsp butter in a medium-sized saucepan over medium heat.

Add 1 clove of chopped garlic and cook for 1 minute.

Add 1 tbsp flour and cook 1 minute. Stir in 1 cup cream, reduce the heat to low, and let simmer until thickened, about 2 minutes.

Stir in ¼ cup Parmesan cheese and season with salt and pepper, to taste.

Alfredo Pizza

INGREDIENTS

12 oz pkg chicken or turkey sausage, cut in bite-size pieces *see note

1 tbsp olive oil

2 cloves garlic, chopped (you can use the garlic in a jar)

1 jar Alfredo sauce (jar sizes range from 15 to 24 oz, pick your favorite brand), or make your own, page 63.

1 roll of pizza dough (find this with canned biscuits and bread dough, or frozen dough products)

2 cups loosely packed fresh spinach, reserve a handful for garnish

1 cup grape or cherry tomatoes (10 to12, grocery store salad bar) cut in halves

1 cup grated Mozzarella cheese

¼ cup grated Parmesan cheese

DIRECTIONS

Preheat oven to 400 degrees.

Heat 1 tbsp of olive oil in a large skillet over medium-high heat. Add sausages and cook until lightly browned.

Add garlic to the skillet right before sausage is done.

On wax paper sprinkled with a little flour, roll out the pizza dough. You can put the dough on a baking sheet, a pizza pan, or a pizza stone if you have one. Who said pizza has to be round? *(hint: Sprinkle the pan with 1 tbsp of cornmeal for a pizza-parlor crunch)*.

Cover the crust with a thin layer of Alfredo sauce.

Top with the spinach, tomatoes, sausage, garlic, and cheese.

Bake until the pizza is crisp and golden, about 25 minutes.

Remove from oven and top with another handful of spinach.

Serves 2 to 4

* Skip sausage to make a delicious **vegetarian pizza.**

Asian Beef and Noodles

(Dinner in 15 minutes.)

INGREDIENTS

8 to 10 oz rib eye steak, sliced in thin strips *(hint: Meat slices easier if you freeze it for about 20 minutes first.)*

1 tbsp sesame oil

1 cup sliced green onions (grocery store salad bar)

14 oz pkg coleslaw mix

2 pkg Ramen noodles, beef flavor

1 tbsp soy sauce

DIRECTIONS

Heat oil in large skillet over medium-high heat, add steak, and stir-fry 1 minute.

Remove steak from the skillet to a platter.

Keeping skillet over medium-high heat, add onions and slaw and stir-fry 1 minute.

Remove slaw mixture from skillet and add to steak.

In the same skillet, boil ¾ cup of water.

Break noodles in half and add to boiling water with 1 sauce packet.

Cook 2 minutes or until water is absorbed, stirring frequently.

Return steak, slaw mixture, and noodles to the skillet.

Add soy sauce and heat thoroughly.

Serves 2 to 3.

Suggestion: Save extra seasoning packet to make a tasty salad dressing. Add seasoning packet, ½ cup vegetable oil, ¼ cup vinegar, and ¼ cup sugar to a clean jar. Shake it up! Dressing will keep in the refrigerator for a week.

Baked Pasta with Italian Sausage

INGREDIENTS

1 tbsp olive oil

12 oz Italian sausage, chicken, turkey or pork, sliced in ¼ inch rounds

1 onion, chopped

28 oz can diced tomatoes

1 tsp dried oregano or Italian seasoning

½ cup half & half

½ tsp salt

⅛ tsp red pepper flakes

1 lb penne pasta, cooked according to package directions

6 oz cheese—pick from Swiss, Fontina, or Gruyere—grate half and cut the rest into ½-inch cubes

¼ cup grated Parmesan cheese

DIRECTIONS

Preheat oven to 350 degrees.

Heat oil in a large skillet over medium heat.

Add sausage and sauté until browned.

Remove sausage from skillet.

Add onion to the same skillet and cook until soft, about 3 minutes.

Stir in tomatoes and oregano; cook until tomatoes are soft, about 15 minutes.

Add half & half and cook until warmed through, about 5 minutes.

Add salt and red pepper flakes. Taste for seasoning.

Add sausage, pasta, and cubed cheese to sauce.

Put in a large casserole dish sprayed with cooking spray.

Top with grated cheese and Parmesan cheese.

Bake until browned and edges are crisp, 30 to 40 minutes.

Serves 6 to 8

Suggestion: If you are 21 or older, add ¼ cup vodka to the sauce when you stir in the tomatoes. Most of the alcohol will cook out of the sauce and leave a wonderful taste. Serve this pasta with a spinach salad topped with red onion, and Italian dressing, recipe page 38, plus a loaf of crusty bread and you have a very lovely meal for either entertaining or a cozy weeknight. Omit sausage, and it's a delicious **vegetarian sauce.**

Beef Stroganoff Nana's Way

I admit this recipe isn't really traditional Beef Stroganoff, but it's what my mother called it and we love this dish. I prepared this recipe all the time when I was in college because it was easy, affordable, and always a crowd pleaser. Once I made the classic Beef Stroganoff for my family and they were furious because this familiar recipe was what they were expecting. So even if you adore a traditional Beef Stroganoff, give this a spin. Whatever you call it, it's delicious!

INGREDIENTS

1 lb ground chuck or lean beef (you could use ground turkey and call it Turkey Stroganoff I suppose)

1 onion, chopped

1 can cream of chicken soup (or make your own, page 62)

1 cup sour cream

1 tsp each, salt and pepper

12 to16 oz pkg wide egg noodles

1 tbsp butter

DIRECTIONS

In a large nonstick skillet, brown beef over medium-high heat. (*hint: Remember that beef won't brown if there is liquid in the pan from the beef. Remove liquid with a spoon.*)

Add onions and sauté until soft. Add salt and pepper.

Stir in soup and heat to simmer, lower heat.

Cook noodles according to package directions. Drain. Add the noodles back to the pan you used to boil them, keeping it off the heat, and toss with butter.

Add sour cream to beef mixture and heat, but don't boil.

Serve over the buttered noodles.

Serves 4

Suggestion: You could serve this on toast instead of noodles for a really easy meal. It's also a great way to use any leftovers.

Brenner Casserole (Breakfast for Dinner)

My family loves to have breakfast for dinner. Pancakes and bacon are a perfect weekday supper when you deserve a reward! This casserole is a great recipe for any meal.

INGREDIENTS

12 to16 link sausages—pork, turkey, or vegetarian—cut in quarters

2 apples, peeled, cored, and thinly sliced

1 box cornbread mix (they vary in size, around 8 oz)

1 egg

⅓ cup milk

DIRECTIONS

Preheat oven to 400 degrees.

Brown sausages in a large skillet over medium-high heat.

Spray an 8 × 8 inch casserole with cooking spray and add the sausages.

Lay apple slices on top.

Mix cornbread mix with milk and egg and pour over the top of the apples and sausage.

Bake for 25 to 30 minutes.

Serve with real maple syrup.

Serves 4

Caramelized Onion Quiche with Bacon

INGREDIENTS

2 onions, chopped (try to find Vidalia onions which are milder and sweeter)

1 tbsp olive oil

½ tsp salt

½ tsp sugar

6 strips of bacon

1 cup half & half or whole milk

⅛ tsp nutmeg

3 eggs

Piecrust *(hint: It's fine to get the frozen ones in aluminum pans, but the piecrusts that you unroll and place in the pan are better and no more trouble if you own a pie pan. Find them with biscuits and cookie dough in the grocery store. Or make your own, page 63.)*

1½ cups grated Gruyere or Swiss cheese

DIRECTIONS

Heat oil in a large skillet over medium-low heat. Add onions, sprinkle with salt and sugar, and cook for 30 minutes or until golden brown and caramelized.

Remove onions from skillet and let cool.

Cook bacon in the same skillet until it is crisp and brown.

Drain on paper towels. Crumble when cooled.

In mixing bowl, whisk together cream, eggs, and, nutmeg.

Add cheese and onion and mix to combine.

Preheat oven to 350 degrees.

Place the crust in a pie pan on a baking sheet.

Put the crumbled bacon on top of the crust.

Pour in filling.

Bake 30 to 35 minutes until just set in the center.

Let cool at least 10 minutes before serving.

Serve warm or at room temperature.

Serves 6 to 8

Suggestion: You could omit bacon for a **vegetarian quiche.** Almost anything you like is delicious in a quiche. Think about mushrooms, ham, asparagus, shrimp, crab…the possibilities are endless!

Definitely a grocery store salad bar moment!

Chicken and Sausage Pie

I have a friend who on occasion asks me to make this for her for parties. She loves to see the women initially put a small serving on their plates, and then all go back for seconds. It can't be helped; this pie is addictive. This is my favorite dish to take to a sick friend who is recuperating at home and needs a healing, hot supper.

INGREDIENTS

1 stick butter

4 tbsp flour

1 cup chicken broth (you can use chicken bouillon cubes)

2 cups half & half or milk

optional: 2 tbsp sherry (you can use cooking sherry found with vinegars in the grocery store)

2 to 3 cups cooked chicken breasts, chopped *see note

½ lb cooked, crumbled, breakfast sausage

½ tsp salt

¼ tsp pepper

Piecrust (hint: *It's fine to get the frozen ones in aluminum pans, but the piecrusts that you unroll and place in the pan are better for this recipe. Find them with biscuits and cookie dough in the grocery store. Or make your own page 63.*)

DIRECTIONS

Preheat oven to 350 degrees.

Make a sauce by melting butter in a medium size saucepan over low heat. Whisk in flour and cook 1 minute, stirring constantly.

Whisk in chicken broth and half & half or milk.

Cook over medium heat until thickened.

Add sherry, if using.

Stir in chicken, sausage, salt, and pepper.

Put in a 9 × 13 casserole dish, or equivalent size (it doesn't have to be a rectangle), and cover with the piecrust. Shape the piecrust to fit the casserole; remember you're the boss of the dish, and you can shape the crust anyway that works.

Pierce several holes in crust with a fork.

Bake for about 30 minutes until crust is golden and filling is bubbly.

Serves 8

* Page 62 has easy directions for cooking chicken.

Chicken Enchiladas

One of my good friends who swears she can't do a thing in the kitchen makes this all the time. I beg to differ; it's just so easy to put together she forgets that she's cooking!

INGREDIENTS

10 oz can green enchilada sauce (in Hispanic section of grocery store)

2½ to 3 cups cooked chicken breast, chopped *see note

8 oz Mexican-blend cheese, grated

¼ cup butter, melted

½ onion, chopped

1 can of cream of chicken or cream of mushroom soup (or make your own, page 63)

4 oz can of chopped green chiles

8 large flour tortillas

2 tbsp canola oil

10 oz can red enchilada sauce

1 cup shredded sharp cheddar cheese

Optional: ¼ cup sliced green onions (grocery store salad bar)

DIRECTIONS

Preheat oven to 400 degrees.

Spray 9 ×13 baking dish with cooking spray and pour in green enchilada sauce.

Combine next 6 ingredients (chicken through chiles) in large bowl.

Remove 1 cup of the chicken mixture and set it aside.

Heat oil in a large skillet over medium heat. Fry both sides of 1 tortilla about 10 seconds. Drain for a few seconds on paper towels.

Fill tortilla with chicken mixture and roll up.

Place filled tortilla, seam side down, in baking dish.

Repeat with remaining 7 tortillas. Add more oil if necessary.

Spread the reserved cup of mixture evenly over the top and then top with red enchilada sauce.

Cover with foil and bake 25 minutes.

Uncover and sprinkle with cheddar cheese and green onions. Bake an extra 10 minutes.

You can make this a day ahead and refrigerate. Bake for 35 minutes.

Serves 4 to 6

* Page 62 has easy directions for cooking chicken.

Chicken Tetrazzini

INGREDIENTS

3 tbsp butter

1 onion, chopped

1 clove garlic, chopped (you can use garlic in the jar)

4 oz mushrooms, sliced

1 tsp each salt and pepper

⅓ cup sherry or white wine (you can use cooking sherry or wine found with vinegars in the grocery store)

½ cup all-purpose flour

2 cups chicken broth (you can use bouillon cubes)

2 cups milk

1½ cups grated Parmesan cheese; save ½ cup for topping

4 oz cream cheese

12 to 16 oz package spaghetti or linguini, cooked according to package directions

2½ to 3 cups cooked chicken breast, chopped *see note

1 slice bread, crumbled to make breadcrumbs

DIRECTIONS

Preheat oven to 350 degrees.

Melt butter in large saucepan or Dutch oven over medium-high heat.

Add onion, garlic, mushrooms, salt, and pepper. Sauté 4 minutes or until tender.

Add sherry and cook 1 minute.

Add flour to pan and cook 2 minutes, stirring constantly.

Gradually add broth and milk, stirring constantly. Bring to a boil.

Reduce heat; simmer 5 minutes, stirring frequently.

Remove from heat and add 1 cup Parmesan cheese and cream cheese, stirring until melted.

Add the pasta and chicken, and stir to blend.

Spray a 9 × 13 casserole with cooking spray; add chicken mixture.

Mix breadcrumbs with ½ cup Parmesan cheese; sprinkle evenly over chicken.

Bake for 30 minutes or until lightly browned.

Serves 8

*Page 62 has easy directions for cooking chicken.

Curry: Chicken or Shrimp

INGREDIENTS

2½ cups cooked chicken breast, chopped *see note; or 2½ cups raw shrimp, peeled and deveined **see note

5 tbsp butter

1 onion, chopped

6 tbsp flour

3 tbsp curry powder

2 cups chicken broth (you can use bouillon cubes)

1 can light coconut milk (in the Asian foods section of the grocery store)

1 tbsp sugar

1 tsp salt

½ tsp ground ginger

1 tbsp lemon juice, fresh or bottled

For serving: rice (The boil-in-the-bag rice is fine. Check servings on the package directions to prepare the amount you will need.)

DIRECTIONS

In a large saucepan, melt butter over medium heat.

Sauté onion until soft, about 5 minutes.

Stir in flour and curry powder and cook 1 minute, stirring constantly.

Add broth and coconut milk and continue to stir until thickened.

Add sugar, salt, and ginger.

Add chicken or shrimp and lemon juice. Heat through.

Serve curry over rice, with as many of the condiments from the list below as you like, or eat as is.

Serves 6 to 8

Optional condiments for a curry are sometimes called the *Seven Sisters*.

They include: peanuts, chopped hard-boiled eggs, coconut flakes, bacon bits (fine from a jar), sliced green onions, raisins, and chutney. I would definitely check the grocery store salad bar for many of these.

*Page 62 has easy directions for cooking chicken.

**Shrimp will cook in hot curry liquid in 3 to 5 minutes depending on the size. They turn pink when

Delicious Salmon Every Time

This recipe is healthy and yummy. It's handy because you can cook it for yourself or a crowd. Best of all, hands-on prep time for the salmon is about five minutes. Leftovers are good the next day on a Caesar salad or in pasta. I'm always hoping for a little bit left on the serving dish. That doesn't often happen.

INGREDIENTS

¼ cup real maple syrup

¼ cup soy sauce

2 cloves garlic, chopped (you can use the garlic in the jar)

1 lb salmon *see note

DIRECTIONS

Combine the first 3 ingredients in a large resealable Baggie, shake it up, and add the salmon.

Marinate in the refrigerator for 1 hour or up to 4 hours.

Preheat the oven to 450 degrees.

Pour the salmon and the marinade into a baking dish, and bake for 12 to 15 minutes, depending on the thickness of the salmon.

You can broil the salmon for about 1 minute if you want a little brown on top, but be careful. More than a minute could make your fish over-cooked.

The salmon is done when it flakes easily at the thickest part.

Serve with the delicious sauce.

Serves 3 to 4

* Don't worry about the skin. Put the salmon skin side down to cook and it peels right off when you take the fish out of the casserole. If you really don't want to deal with the skin, most butchers will take it off if you ask, or use a knife to remove it before cooking.

Serving Suggestion: This is great with couscous, page 85 or quinoa, page 82, and the Asian Salad, page 40.

Dirty Rice Casserole

This recipe was a stop-the-presses moment in real life. My son was looking through the final version of this cookbook, ready to be sent off to the printer, and he said, "Where's the Dirty Rice recipe? It has to be in the cookbook." Well here's my dirty little secret; I really don't have a recipe, and I just throw stuff together! So he and I experimented until we decided it was just right, and this is the end result. We like the slight crunch the rice retains, plus the little bit of heat. Need I say it's one of his favorite dishes?

INGREDIENTS

1½ lb lean ground beef or turkey

1 tsp olive or canola oil

1 onion, chopped

1 bell pepper, red, yellow, or green, chopped

4 cloves garlic, chopped (fresh is best in this recipe)

1 can cream of mushroom soup (or make your own, page 62)

1 can cream of celery soup (or make your own, page 62)

2 boxes of dirty rice mix (traditional spicy Cajun rice, found with rice mixes in the grocery store)

1 cup water

Optional: hot sauce

DIRECTIONS

Preheat oven to 325 degrees.

Brown beef or turkey in a large skillet coated with oil over medium-high heat *(hint: Remember that meat won't brown if there is liquid in the pan from the meat. Remove liquid with a spoon.)*

When meat is browned, add onion, pepper, and garlic, and cook until soft, about 5 minutes.

In a mixing bowl, combine meat mixture with the soups, water, and the two packages of uncooked dirty rice including any seasoning packets that come with the rice mixes. Add a little hot sauce if you want this really spicy.

Spray a 9 × 13 casserole with cooking spray and add meat mixture.

Cover tightly with foil and bake for 2 hours.

Serves 6 to 8

Serving Suggestion: This is really good with the Tomato Dressing and Steak Sauce, page 59. Dirty Rice is also yummy with red beans. Canned pinto or red beans can be drained and heated in a small saucepan with a bit of Cajun seasoning or hot sauce to taste. Serve on the side sprinkled with a little chopped green onion as a garnish. (grocery store salad bar)

Fish in Foil

This recipe is a fabulous way to cook fish and it's completely foolproof! Baking fish in parchment paper or tin foil—known in France and gourmet kitchens as *en papillote*—steams the fish with a minimum of fuss and equipment. You probably already have aluminum foil in your kitchen, but you could use parchment for a very elegant presentation. Either way, you'll love the clean healthy taste of this dish.

INGREDIENTS

2 mild fish filets, good choices are tilapia, sea bass, orange roughy, or snapper (not so great for darker fish like tuna or salmon)

4 slices of onion

4 slices of tomato

2 tbsp butter

1 tsp Cajun seasoning, blackened fish seasoning, or a mix of salt, pepper, and cayenne pepper

2 lemon slices

DIRECTIONS

Preheat oven to 400 degrees.

Cut 2 pieces of aluminum foil or parchment paper (found with foil and other paper products in the grocery store) about ¾ the size of a baking sheet.

Lay 2 slices of onion and 2 slices of tomato on one side of each rectangle of foil or paper.

Put fish on top.

Sprinkle each piece of fish with about ½ tsp of seasoning.

Top with lemon.

Put 1 tbsp butter on top of each piece of fish. (It melts while cooking to form the sauce.)

Fold up foil or paper squares tightly.

Place on a baking sheet and bake for 15 minutes.

For presentation, serve in the foil or paper with scissors to cut it open at the table.

Serves 2

Serving Suggestion: The sauce this makes while it cooks is delicious. Serve with potatoes, rice, or quinoa, Bonus Recipe, p 82, to soak it all up.

Bonus Recipe: Quinoa

Bring 2 cups water to boil. Add 1 tsp salt or alternately add 2 chicken bouillon cubes for flavor, and 1 cup of dry quinoa. (find quinoa with rice and pasta in the grocery store)

Stir, cover with lid, and cook over low heat for 15 minutes.

I throw a small handful (about 2 to 3 tbsp) of raisins or dried cranberries in my quinoa before I put on the lid. I like the taste and texture. You could add 2 tbsp green onions and/or toasted almonds as well. This is also good cold by itself or in a salad.

Fresh Tomato Spaghetti

Because this recipe relies on cherry tomatoes, which taste good all year long, you can have this dish in the middle of winter when you're just dreaming of summer.

INGREDIENTS

1 pint of cherry or grape tomatoes

1 tbsp olive oil

½ tsp each, salt, sugar, and pepper

6 oz spaghetti

2 oz ricotta salata or feta cheese *see note

Dried or fresh basil, about 1 tsp dried or 5 or 6 leaves fresh, chopped or torn

DIRECTIONS

Preheat oven to 400 degrees.

Cut tomatoes in half and put on a foil-lined pan *(hint: I use my pie pan. It's the perfect size.)*

Toss with olive oil, salt, sugar, and pepper and bake for 20 minutes.

Cook pasta according to package directions.

Drain, saving ¼ cup of cooking water.

Put drained pasta back in pan. Add tomatoes, reserved water, fresh or dried basil, and crumbled cheese. Toss and enjoy!

Serves 2

*There are certainly other cheeses that you could substitute. Both of these are very crumbly and salty. You are the boss of your kitchen and can experiment with other tastes and textures.

Suggestion: This could also be a side dish for a simple grilled or broiled fish (next recipe) or pan-seared chicken.

A Simple Way to Cook a Fish

The original cookbook for my son didn't contain any fish recipes because he doesn't eat a lot of fish. He says that fish are his friends. Clearly he's not so tight with pigs and cows. I don't get it and keep trying to change his mind. I do suspect that some cooks, even more experienced ones, are intimidated by the idea of cooking fish. This recipe makes it very easy. Maybe it will even convert my son.

INGREDIENTS

Any fish: cod, salmon, halibut, sea bass, tilapia—pick one you like or that is on sale, about 6 oz for each person you are serving

1 tbsp canola oil

Salt and pepper

DIRECTIONS

Heat oil in a nonstick or cast iron skillet that has a lid, over medium-high heat until very hot.

Salt and pepper both sides of fish and put in heated pan.

Cook until golden brown on one side, about 2 minutes.

Turn fish and cover skillet with a tight fitting lid.

Remove from heat and let the steam do the work cooking your fish.

An average 1-inch thick piece should be done in about 10 minutes.

A squeeze of lemon is nice but not necessary.

Serves 1

Suggestion: This is a superb **dinner for one** or just for a very busy day. With a salad or steamed veggies and quick-cooking couscous, you can have dinner in 15 minutes.

Bonus Recipe: Couscous

Bring 1¼ cups water to boil. Add ½ tsp salt or alternately add a chicken bouillon cube for flavor, and 1 cup of dry couscous. (find it with rice and pasta in the grocery store)

Stir, cover with lid, and remove from heat for 5 minutes.

Remove lid and fluff with a fork.

I throw a small handful (about 2 to 3 tbsp) of raisins or dried cranberries in my couscous before I put on the lid. I like the taste and texture. You could add 2 tbsp green onions and/or toasted almonds as well.

Italian Sausage Sandwiches

I never have to ask my son what he wants me to cook for game day during football season, because this is always the answer.

INGREDIENTS

2 tbsp olive oil

1 lb Italian turkey or chicken sausage, casings removed, cut in 2-inch pieces lengthwise

2 bell peppers, red, green, or yellow or a combo, sliced

1 onion, sliced into rings

2 cloves garlic, chopped (you can use the garlic in a jar)

1 tsp each, salt and pepper

½ tsp oregano or Italian seasoning

2 tbsp tomato paste *(hint: You can use pizza or spaghetti sauce.)*

½ cup Marsala or other wine (you can use cooking wine found with vinegars in the grocery store) or chicken broth or water

¼ tsp red pepper flakes or a dash of hot sauce

For serving: 4 Italian or French bread rolls

DIRECTIONS

Heat oil in a large skillet over medium heat and cook sausages until brown, about 10 minutes. Remove sausages from skillet.

Keep the skillet over medium heat; add the peppers, onions, salt, and pepper, and cook until golden brown, about 5 minutes.

Add the oregano or Italian seasoning and garlic, and cook 2 more minutes.

Add the tomato paste and stir.

Add the wine and red pepper flakes.

Stir to combine, scraping the skillet to release all the browned bits. Bring to a simmer.

Add the sausages back to the skillet and stir to combine.

Cook until the sauce has thickened, about 20 minutes.

Serves 4

To serve: Split the rolls in half lengthwise. Hollow out a little bread from the bottom side of each roll.

Fill the bottom half of the roll with sausage mixture.

Replace tops and serve the sandwiches immediately.

Mandarin Orange Chicken

(Dinner in 15 minutes)

I invented this dish for my son who has had an insane love affair with mandarin oranges since he was very young. I don't understand it but what the heck, there are worse addictions. Not that he has noticed, but this is a pretty dish too. In his words, "If it tastes good, it's all good."

INGREDIENTS

1 lb chicken-breast tenders or chicken breasts cut in 1-inch pieces (Rinse chicken first—remember clean work surface and clean hands.)

¾ tsp each, salt and pepper

1 tbsp butter

1 tbsp olive oil

½ cup orange marmalade

1 tbsp cornstarch

7 oz can mandarin oranges, drained

Optional: sesame seeds and sliced green onion (grocery store salad bar) for garnish

DIRECTIONS

Sprinkle chicken with salt and pepper.

Heat butter and oil in a large nonstick skillet over medium-high heat.

Add chicken to the skillet and cook 4 minutes or until lightly browned.

Combine orange marmalade and cornstarch in a small bowl.

Gently stir in oranges.

Add marmalade mixture to the skillet; cover and simmer 6 minutes or until the sauce is slightly thick, stirring once.

Sprinkle with sesame seeds and sliced green onions if desired.

Serves 3

Serving suggestion: Stir chopped cashews and raisins into hot, cooked, boil- in-the-bag rice for a speedy side dish.

Meatloaf: Beef or Turkey

Everyone loves a good meatloaf, but here's a secret: this recipe is so flavorful my family can't tell if it's made with beef or turkey. Whatever your preference, this makes a delicious meatloaf. If you are cooking for one or two, mix up the ingredients for the meatloaf (meat through Worcestershire sauce) and freeze half for a later date. Or enjoy tasty leftovers – suggestion below.

INGREDIENTS

2 lb ground beef or turkey (don't use 99 percent fat-free turkey; meatloaf needs a little fat)

1 cup bread crumbs (about 6 slices torn up) soaked in 1 cup milk, buttermilk, or water for 5 minutes

1 egg beaten

½ onion, chopped

2 cloves garlic, chopped (you can use garlic in the jar)

1 tsp oregano

1½ tsp salt

½ tsp pepper

1 tbsp Worcestershire sauce *(hint: You can substitute soy sauce.)*

½ cup brown sugar

1 cup ketchup

1 tsp mustard

Optional: 4 to 6 slices of bacon

DIRECTIONS

Preheat oven to 350 degrees.

Squeeze most of the liquid from bread and mix with meat, egg, onion, garlic, oregano, salt and pepper, and Worcestershire sauce.

Form into a loaf shape and put in a rimmed pan lined with foil.

Mix ketchup, sugar, and mustard and spread over meatloaf.

Top with bacon, if using. Bake for 1 hour and 15 minutes.

Serves 6

Suggestion: Leftovers are delicious cold! Makes an incredible sandwich—bread, lettuce, tomato, mayo, and sliced meatloaf.

Serving Suggestion: For a party you can bake meat mixture in muffin tins for individual servings. Everyone likes this because there are more crispy edges! This is perfect with Potatoes au Gratin, page 122 and frozen green peas cooked in the microwave in water with a little butter plus a tablespoon of sherry if you have it.

New Orleans Barbeque Shrimp

THE STORY

I swear this dish tastes better when you know the story of how I got the recipe. I was in New Orleans waiting in line at the dry cleaners. I was at the dry cleaners because of an unfortunate accident the night before involving a very inebriated person at a Mardi Gras parade. Waiting in line with me was a charming older lady who asked if I knew how to make Barbeque Shrimp. When I said that I did not, she recited this recipe from memory. She told me it was her favorite dish and an old family secret. I don't know what inspired her to make me the lucky recipient of the recipe, but I couldn't wait to get home and make it. When we were younger, my friends called it "the boyfriend catcher"! I think it could also be "the girlfriend catcher" if used appropriately by a handsome gentleman.

INGREDIENTS

2 lb shrimp, shell on

2 onions, sliced into rings

5 tbsp pepper

5 tbsp paprika

1 bottle Italian dressing, not fat free

1 stick butter

For serving: French bread

DIRECTIONS

Preheat the oven to 350 degrees.

Put onions, Italian dressing, butter, pepper, and paprika in a large casserole dish. Bake for 5 minutes, and then stir to distribute butter. Bake 10 more minutes. Add shrimp and stir to coat with sauce.

Bake about 10 to 15 minutes, depending on the size of your shrimp, until they turn pink and are done.

Serves 6

Serving Suggestion: Cover your table with newspaper. Put the pan of shrimp in the middle of the table on a towel or trivet. Serve with French bread and let your guests or family make a mess throwing peels on paper and using bread to dip in the sauce and onions. For clean up, you throw away the paper and wash the pan! How easy is that?

Richard's Favorite Pasta

One night I was trying to think of what to make for a last-minute dinner. Richard was staring morosely into the refrigerator waiting for something to suddenly look delicious. He said he wanted some pasta with Alfredo sauce and then spotted a package of Italian turkey sausage. Viola! This recipe is Richard's masterpiece.

INGREDIENTS

1 tbsp olive oil

12 to 16 oz pkg mild Italian turkey sausage, casings removed, cut in 1-inch pieces

4 large cloves garlic, chopped

1 tsp fennel seeds

¼ cup white wine (you can use cooking wine found with vinegars in the grocery store)

1 jar Alfredo sauce (Or homemade if you are making this for a person who is already terribly spoiled. Alfredo Sauce, recipe page 63.) Jar sizes range from 15 to 24 oz, so use your favorite brand.

For serving: 12 oz package pasta of choice - rotini or penne are good choices, cooked according to package directions

Optional: grated Parmesan cheese for topping.

DIRECTIONS

Heat oil in a large skillet over medium-high heat.

Add sausage and cook until well browned about 10 minutes.

Add garlic and sauté until soft, 2 minutes.

Add fennel seeds and wine and cook until wine evaporates.

Stir in Alfredo sauce and heat through.

Serve on pasta.

Serves 4

Serving Suggestion: Serve with a simple salad of romaine lettuce with cherry tomatoes and sliced red onions (grocery salad bar) and Italian dressing, recipe page 38. Include sorbet for dessert and you've got yourself an elegant little dinner party!

Spaghetti Sauce

We have a lot of food traditions in our family that I have learned not to mess with. Probably the most important is spaghetti for dinner the first night at the beach—any beach. It's like turkey at Thanksgiving or champagne on New Year's Eve. Once we went to Navarre Beach, and I made chili the first night. My family gave me the silent treatment for days. When I was growing up my mom made spaghetti every Sunday night. We may not be on a schedule, but we sure do love this spaghetti sauce and manage to have spaghetti for dinner frequently, even though I agree that it tastes best at the beach!
What doesn't?

INGREDIENTS

1 lb ground beef or turkey

1 tbsp olive oil

1 onion, chopped

2 cloves garlic, chopped (you can use garlic in a jar)

1 tsp of each, oregano, basil (Italian seasoning can be substituted)

1½ tsp salt

⅛ tsp red pepper flakes

6 oz can of tomato paste

8 oz can tomato sauce

14.5 oz can diced tomatoes

½ cup red wine (you can use cooking wine found with vinegars in the grocery store)

1 tsp sugar or to taste (it cuts the acidity from tomatoes)

Optional: 1 bay leaf

For serving: 12 oz pkg spaghetti, cooked according to package directions and grated Parmesan cheese.

DIRECTIONS

Brown meat in oil *(hint: If there is a lot of liquid in the pan that comes from the meat as it heats, it will not brown so remove the liquid with a spoon.)*

Add onion and garlic to beef and cook until soft, about 5 minutes.

While the vegetables cook; open all cans and have ready.

Add oregano, basil, salt, and red pepper flakes, and stir for about 30 seconds.

Add tomatoes, tomato paste, tomato sauce, wine, sugar, and bay leaf, if using.

The sauce is much better simmered for an hour or two and sometimes needs more liquid. Wine, broth, or even water is fine.

Serve on spaghetti noodles with lots of Parmesan cheese.

Serves 4

Bonus Recipe: Garlic Bread

Preheat oven to 400 degrees. Split a loaf of French or Italian bread in half horizontally and place cut sides up on a baking sheet. Mix one stick of softened butter with 4 garlic cloves, minced and spread on bread. Bake for 15 minutes. Remove from oven and turn oven to broil. Mix together ¼ c each of Parmesan and Mozzarella cheese and top bread. Broil 1 to 2 minutes to lightly brown the tops.

Spicy Mongolian Beef or Chicken

INGREDIENTS

1 lb sirloin or chicken, sliced thin *(hint: If you put beef in the freezer for about 20 minutes, it's easier to slice)*

½ cup soy sauce

2 tbsp sherry or rice wine (cooking sherry from the grocery store is with vinegars, and rice wine with Asian foods)

2 tsp sesame oil

2 tbsp cornstarch

3 tbsp sugar

½ tsp crushed red pepper flakes

3 tbsp vegetable oil

1 cup sliced green onions (grocery store salad bar)

DIRECTIONS

Combine soy sauce, sherry, sesame oil, cornstarch, sugar, and pepper flakes in a medium-sized bowl. Add meat and refrigerate for 20 minutes.

Heat 1 tbsp oil in large skillet over medium-high heat.

Add green onions and stir-fry until tender, about 5 minutes.

Remove from skillet.

Add remaining 2 tbsp of oil to the skillet and heat to medium-high.

Add beef with marinade and stir-fry 5 minutes until done.

Add onions and serve on noodles or rice.

Serves 4

Serving Suggestion: I had a similar dish in the only cooking class I've ever taken. The instructor, who was actually from China, served this on fried bean thread noodles. It was spectacular. You can find the dried noodles in the Asian foods section of any grocery store. They come wrapped up as "nests." You don't need to pull the noodles apart.

Heat about 3 inches of vegetable oil in a pot only large enough to hold noodles. When it is really hot (you can test by dropping in one noodle), add noodles in one big lump, just the way they come out of the package. As they puff up, use tongs to turn over and almost immediately remove from pan to paper towels. This only takes about 1 minute. Sprinkle with a little salt and serve. If you want to reuse the oil to fry something else, let it cool and put it in a jar. Keep the jar in the refrigerator.

Taco Pizza

There is a funny story about this dish. My son's best friend just adores Taco Pizza and when he comes to visit or travels with us, I always make it for him. Once, when we were vacationing in the Smoky Mountains, I made several pizzas and we enjoyed the leftovers the next day. The following morning I put small pieces of leftover pizza dough on the porch railing for the birds. I looked out of the window and there was my son's friend, (he chooses to remain nameless for obvious reasons) walking along eating the pizza off the railing. I would have been truly horrified if I had been able to stop laughing! But hey, that's a pretty good endorsement for any recipe.

INGREDIENTS

1 loaf frozen white bread dough, thawed *(hint: Put it on wax paper sprayed with cooking spray and leave it alone for at least 6 hours.)*

1 lb ground turkey

1 tbsp olive or canola oil

1 pkg taco seasoning

12 to 16 oz jar of salsa

1 cup shredded cheddar cheese

Optional garnishes: lettuce, chopped tomato, black olives, sour cream, extra cheese, avocado (grocery store salad bar)

DIRECTIONS

Preheat oven to 450 degrees.

Roll out dough to fit a 9 × 13 pan or a pizza pan or baking sheet sprayed with cooking spray. Who says a pizza has to be round? *(hint: Sprinkle the pan with 1 tbsp of cornmeal first for that authentic pizza-parlor crunch.)*

Heat oil in a large skillet over medium-high heat, add turkey, and cook until browned, stirring to crumble.

Add taco seasoning and salsa.

Cook for about 5 minutes to blend seasoning.

Top dough with turkey mixture then top with cheese.

Bake for 20 to 25 minutes.

Serve with any garnishes you choose.

Serves 4

THE Casserole

We call this "THE Casserole," and there is a reason for that. Richard has a friend from the West Coast, where I now know, casseroles are not on the menu. She was coming to dinner and Richard told her we were having a casserole. When we sat down to eat, she politely said, "I love casserole. It's one of my favorites." This sounded sort of weird until we realized she had never had a casserole, or heard of one, and imagined it as another bizarre food unique to the South like grits or fried green tomatoes. She assumed that this one dish was the thing we called "casserole." We explained that there are different casseroles with different ingredients, but for her, this is THE casserole, and we can't fob her off with anything else.

INGREDIENTS

2½ to 3 cups cooked chicken, chopped *see note

1 pkg wild and long rice mix

1 can cream of celery soup (or make your own, page 62)

1 onion, chopped

1 cup mayonnaise (the kind made with olive oil is healthier)

2 (16 oz) cans French style green beans, rinsed to get rid of can taste

8 oz can water chestnuts rinsed and chopped (find in the grocery store with Asian foods)

Salt and pepper to taste (rice mix and soup have salt so just taste)

Optional: paprika to sprinkle over the top before baking

DIRECTIONS

Preheat oven to 350 degrees.

Cook wild rice mixture with 2 cups water and seasoning packet. *(hint: If you poached your chicken, use the leftover broth.)*

Mix with all other ingredients except paprika.

Place in a 9 × 13 casserole, sprayed lightly with cooking spray, and sprinkled with paprika, if using it.

Bake for 30 minutes.

Serves 8

*Page 62 has easy directions for cooking chicken.

Serving Suggestion: Easy to make ahead and refrigerate until time to bake.

Your Mama's Chili

This is our house chili and we've been making it just this way for years. People frequently ask for the recipe and are surprised by the secret ingredient. You may be reading the list of ingredients and thinking, "Chocolate in chili? That's crazy!" When I went to Mexico, I fell in love with a chicken dish that had a mole sauce made with chocolate and spicy peppers. It's true that chocolate has been a part of Mexican cooking in savory dishes for centuries. I'm extremely glad someone figured out how to add sugar, but chocolate adds a little something special to many Mexican savory dishes, including this chili.

INGREDIENTS

2 lb ground beef or turkey

1 onion, chopped

1 tbsp canola or olive oil

1 pkg chili seasoning

1 pkg taco seasoning

24 oz jar picante sauce

14.5 oz can diced tomatoes, drained

15 oz can black beans, drained (you can also use kidney beans)

15 oz can chili beans with sauce

Chocolate, either ½ square unsweetened or a tbsp of semisweet chips

Optional, but not at college: beer about ½ cup, or Jack Daniel's ¼ cup

DIRECTIONS

In a large pot or Dutch Oven, brown meat in oil. *(hint: If there is a lot of liquid in the pan that comes from the meat as it heats, the meat will not brown so remove the liquid with a spoon.)*

Add onion and sauté until soft about 5 minutes. *(hint: at this point you could add meat, onions, and remaining ingredients to a Crock-Pot and cook on Low for six hours).*

Open jars and cans to have ready.

Stir in both packages of seasoning and cook for about 30 seconds.

Add remaining ingredients and simmer as long as you want to, but at least an hour. Add water if it gets too dry.

Serves 6 to 8

Leftover Suggestion: Day 2, Chili Dogs—Day 3, Chili Pie

Chili Pie: Put leftover chili in a casserole, topped with grated cheddar cheese and prepared corn muffin mix. Bake at 350 for 25 minutes.

Very Quick Chicken and Dumplings

This is a basic recipe that you can play around with. You could try any variety of vegetables, or add a dash of sherry or white wine. My son always sautés lots of sliced carrots for his version. I would put mushrooms in mine, but then my family would turn up their collective noses. Just like the hamburger folks say, "Have it your way."

INGREDIENTS

1 rotisserie chicken, meat shredded (you could cook your own chicken, which is fine, but would take more time) *see note

1½ cups frozen peas or frozen mixed vegetables, or any cooked veggies you choose to add

1 can cream of chicken soup (or make your own page 62)

1 cup milk

¼ tsp dried thyme or poultry seasoning

½ tsp each, salt and pepper

1 roll of refrigerated biscuits or one pkg frozen biscuits **see note

DIRECTIONS

Preheat oven to 400 degrees.

Combine the chicken, peas or mixed vegetables, soup, milk, poultry seasoning or thyme, and salt and pepper in a large bowl.

Transfer the mixture to an 8 × 8 or similar size casserole, sprayed with cooking spray.

Cover with foil, and bake for 15 minutes.

Remove foil.

Place the biscuits on top of the casserole, pushing them into the sauce a little, and bake until the biscuits are golden brown and cooked through, about 15 to 20 minutes.

Serves 4 to 6

*Page 62 has easy directions for cooking chicken

**You can also make Bisquick biscuits following the package directions and drop the dough on top by the spoonful.

Hearty Potato Soup, p. 111, Easiest Rolls, p. 138, Chicken Tortilla Soup, p. 107

INTRODUCTION TO

Crock-Pot/Slow Cooker Recipes

A somewhat successful attempt has been made to refer to Crock-Pots as slow cookers, since *Crock-Pot* was the original brand name. I guess that's meant to sound more sophisticated, but when I was growing up everyone called them Crock-Pots, which seemed just fine. I love to cook this way so much that I should be ashamed to admit that I own three Crock-Pots, but I'm just not. They are quite inexpensive at large retail stores and now, even in the grocery store. Crock-Pots last forever—one of mine just celebrated a twenty-fifth birthday!

A Crock-Pot was the first cooking appliance that Richard requested. He remembers how very satisfying it was for us to all come home after a long day at work and school and open the door to the most heavenly smells on earth. Once a contractor who was building our porch asked me if I was trying to kill his crew because of the irresistible smell of Beef Stew, page 105, wafting out the door. I had to promise them leftovers for lunch the next day. That is one of many great things about a Crock-Pot meal—you are guaranteed leftovers unless you invite a crowd over for dinner. I could easily cook for a month in my Crock-Pot and barely miss the stove. It has proven invaluable for entertaining. I've hosted many a Super Bowl Sunday for friends who know that two Crock-Pots full of chili were just waiting to be devoured, Your Mama's Chili, page 99. Make it ahead and keep warm in the Crock-Pot. French Dip Sandwiches, page 110, are always a Game Day hit.

Here's a warning—just reading these recipes can make you hungry. They are all family favorites. There are a lot of recipes out there that require tons of prep work before the food goes in the Crock-Pot, but I ignore those. The whole purpose is to be able to quickly toss in the ingredients, cover the Crock-Pot, turn it to the correct setting, and know that in eight hours at the most you will have produced something wonderful. When I have to be out of the door by 7:00 a.m., I put the ingredients in the Crock-Pot the night before and stick the whole thing in my fridge to start in the morning. The hardest part is convincing my family not to peek when they get home. If you take the lid off while cooking you release steam and heat.

Don't overlook the two desserts. Heavenly! Stock up on ice cream.

Take my advice and make the beef stew first. If you're not married, someone will likely propose to you.

Aunt Mary's Crock-Pot Barbecue

Don't you think it would be entertaining to tell people that your barbecue sauce has a soft drink in it? My sister discovered this recipe and her guys request it all the time. I'm a barbecue snob who spent many years in Memphis and I really like this recipe too. It's great for entertaining. I added the onions because I love the flavor, but feel free to leave them out if you're not an onion person. Directions for an unsauced pulled pork follow.

INGREDIENTS

3 to 3½ lb pork shoulder or roast

2 onions, peeled and quartered

1 can real Coke

18 oz bottle of barbecue sauce *see note

Optional: 1 tsp liquid smoke and/or hot sauce to taste

DIRECTIONS

Put the onions in the bottom of the Crock-Pot.

Put pork on top.

Pour Coke and barbecue sauce over.

Add liquid smoke and/or hot sauce, if using

Cook on Low for 8 hours.

Remove from Crock-Pot, and shred with a fork.

Skim any accumulated fat from the sauce; return pork to sauce and serve on cornbread or buns.

Serves 8

*If you wanted **pulled pork** that wasn't already in a barbecue sauce, here's the trick. Give the pork a dry rub by mixing together 4 tbsp paprika, 1 tsp each garlic salt and cumin, and ½ tsp cayenne pepper. Cover the pork with the spice mixture, rubbing it into the meat. Refrigerate rubbed pork for 1 hour or overnight. Follow the same directions, but substitute 2 cups each of apple cider and chicken broth for the Coke and barbeque sauce.

Serving Suggestion: You can put meat without sauce or liquid in a casserole or on a baking sheet and broil in the oven to get some crispy browned pieces.

Beef Stew: My Best Crock-Pot Recipe

INGREDIENTS

2 to 3 lb beef roast (rump, bottom sirloin, chuck, eye of round—whatever is on sale) 1
can mushroom soup (or make your own, page 62)

1 pkg French onion soup mix

1 soup can red wine (you can use cooking wine found with vinegars in the grocery store)
or apple juice, or water

OPTIONAL: ROASTED VEGETABLES

2 or 3 carrots

1 onion

2 baking potatoes or 4 or 5 small new potatoes

2 tbsp olive oil

Salt and pepper

DIRECTIONS

Put roast in Crock-Pot.

Mix soups and wine and pour over roast.

Cook on High for 7 to 8 hours.

Serves 6

FOR OPTIONAL VEGETABLES:

Preheat oven to 400 degrees.

About an hour before serving, peel and slice carrots, quarter unpeeled potatoes, and quarter onion.

Line a baking sheet with foil, add vegetables, and toss with olive oil, salt, and pepper.

Bake until brown with crispy edges.

No time for that? Make baked potatoes, page 117.

Shred roast and serve with vegetables and all of that fabulous sauce.

WHAT TO DO WITH LEFTOVERS

If you have leftovers you can put the beef with any leftover vegetables and sauce in a casserole. Add frozen peas if you have them. Cover with a purchased piecrust, or make your own page 63, and bake for 30 minutes in a 350-degree oven or until crust is brown and sauce is bubbling.

Now you have **Beef Potpie.** Lucky you!

Chicken Cordon Bleu

Once I made this recipe using brightly colored wooden toothpicks, and ended up with an odd bluish-green sauce. It was a conversation starter, but not the most attractive presentation. Look for natural wood toothpicks.

INGREDIENTS

4 chicken breasts

4 slices of ham

4 slices of Swiss cheese

1 can cream of chicken or cream of mushroom soup (or make your own, page 62)

¼ cup white wine (you can use cooking wine found with vinegars in the grocery store) or water

Wooden toothpicks (in baking section of grocery store)

DIRECTIONS

Put chicken between layers of wax paper and pound out to about 1-inch thick. (I use my rolling pin, but a heavy pot will work. Rinse chicken first—remember clean work surface and clean hands.)

Put one slice of ham and one slice of cheese on each chicken breast.

Roll up with chicken on outside and secure with a toothpick. (use 2 if you need to)

Mix soup with water or wine.

Put chicken in the Crock-Pot and cover with soup mixture.

Cook on Low for 6 hours or High for 4 hours.

Serve with sauce.

Serves 4

Suggestion: This is perfect to make the night before a busy day. This recipe can be assembled the night before and left in the refrigerator until you start your Crock-Pot the next day.

Serving Suggestion: This is delicious on toasted French bread, with rice or pasta, or even on mashed potatoes.

Chicken Tortilla Soup

INGREDIENTS

1 to 1½ lb chicken breasts, cut in 1-inch cubes (Rinse chicken first—remember clean work surface and clean hands.) *see note

14.5 oz can diced tomatoes, undrained

10 oz can mild red enchilada sauce

1 onion, chopped

4 oz can chopped green chiles, undrained

4 cups chicken broth

1 tsp cumin

1 tbsp chili powder

1 bay leaf

10 to 12 oz pkg frozen corn

Optional: 1 tbsp chopped cilantro

For serving: 5 corn tortillas, or purchased tortilla chips

DIRECTIONS

Add all ingredients except tortillas to Crock-Pot. Stir to combine.

Cook on Low for 8 hours or High for 6 hours.

Serves 8 to 10

TORTILLAS

Cut the corn tortillas into 1-inch wide strips, toss with a little olive or canola oil, put on a baking sheet, and bake in a 400-degree oven for about 5 minutes.

You can use purchased tortilla chips.

Optional Garnishes: shredded cheese, diced avocado, chopped cilantro, sour cream, and/or sliced green onions

*Omit chicken and substitute vegetable broth for the chicken broth for a delicious **vegetarian soup.**

Crock-Pot Cherry Cobbler

Let your Crock-Pot do the work next time you want a warm and satisfying dessert. Your friends will be amazed when you serve dessert from a Crock-Pot. Plus the smell is over the top!

INGREDIENTS

2 (18 to 21 oz) cans cherry pie filling

1 egg, beaten

3 tbsp milk

3 tbsp butter, melted

½ tsp cinnamon

¼ tsp nutmeg

1 yellow cake mix

For serving: ice cream

DIRECTIONS

Spray the Crock-Pot with cooking spray.

Place pie filling in Crock-Pot and cook on High for 30 minutes.

While it cooks, combine egg, milk, butter, cinnamon, and nutmeg in a large bowl, mixing thoroughly.

Stir the cake mix into the egg mixture until crumbly and spoon on top of the hot pie filling.

Cover and cook for 2 to 3 hours on Low.

Serve warm with ice cream.

Serves 8

Delicious Chicken and Bacon

INGREDIENTS

4 boneless chicken breasts

¼ cup flour

½ cup sour cream

4 slices bacon

1 can cream of mushroom soup (or make your own, page 62)

1 clove garlic, chopped (you can use garlic in a jar)

DIRECTIONS

Wrap a slice of bacon around each chicken breast, sprinkle with a little salt and pepper and place in the Crock-Pot.

Mix together the flour, sour cream, soup, and garlic until well blended.

Pour this mixture over the bacon-wrapped chicken.

Cook for 7 to 8 hours on Low.

Serves 4

Serving Suggestion: This is one of the easiest Crock-Pot recipes, and it makes your house smell amazing. It's a breeze to double for a crowd. Serve with rice or noodles or my favorite, mashed potatoes. This is another great recipe to assemble the night before a busy day and store in the fridge overnight.

VARIATION

Before you add chicken, spray the Crock-Pot with cooking spray and add a box of wild and long grain rice mix, sprinkle with ½ of the seasoning packet and ½ cup of water.

Top that with a jar of chipped beef, cut in small pieces (find this with tuna and canned meats in the grocery store) *(hint: Use kitchen scissors to cut beef)*.

Follow original recipe directions, adding the remaining rice seasoning in the packet to the sour cream mixture before you pour it over the chicken.

Cook for 7 to 8 hours on Low.

Now you have what we called **"Party Chicken."**

French Dip Sandwiches

INGREDIENTS

2 to 3 lb beef roast (rump, bottom sirloin, eye of round—whatever is on sale!)

1 pkg French onion soup mix

2 cups beef broth

1 beer, you can use the nonalcoholic kind or 12 oz of apple juice

1 tbsp steak seasoning

French rolls

Butter—1 tbsp for each roll

Optional: horseradish sauce, Swiss or Provolone cheese

DIRECTIONS

Place roast in Crock-Pot.

Add the beef broth, onion soup, beer or apple juice, and seasoning.

Cook on Low for 7 hours.

Preheat oven to 350 degrees.

Split French rolls, and spread with butter.

Bake 10 minutes.

Shred meat and place on the rolls.

Serve the sauce on the side for dipping along with horseradish sauce and cheese if desired.

Serves 6 to 8

Serving Suggestion: This is delicious with Sweet Potato Fries, page 127.

Hearty Potato Soup

INGREDIENTS

6 potatoes, peeled and cut into ½-inch cubes

2 onions, diced

2 carrots, peeled and thinly sliced

2 ribs celery, thinly sliced

4 cups chicken broth (you can use 4 bouillon cubes)

1 tsp dried basil

1 tsp each, salt and pepper

¼ cup flour

1½ cups half & half

DIRECTIONS

Combine first 7 ingredients in a Crock-Pot.

Cook on High 3 hours or Low 6 hours until vegetables are tender.

Mix flour and half & half together in a small bowl and stir into soup.

Cover and cook on high 30 minutes or until heated through and thick.

Serves 6

Serving Suggestion: Serve with cheese, bacon bits, and chopped green onion on top to make it even better. Delicious with the Easiest Rolls, recipe page 138.

Suggestion: For a cheesier version you can stir in ½ cup of shredded cheddar cheese for the last 15 minutes of cooking.

Rice Stuffed Turkey Breast

This is a great way to have an excellent meal and really tasty leftovers. Who says turkey is only for holidays? You could use leftover turkey in any of the recipes that call for chopped, cooked chicken. This turkey is so tender that it can be sliced to make wonderful sandwiches. Of course you could just host a small party for three or four friends and wish you had those leftovers the next day. Add some steamed green beans for a beautiful, healthy, and cost-friendly dinner.

INGREDIENTS

2 boxes wild and long grain rice blend

1 onion, chopped

$\frac{1}{2}$ cup dried cranberries

1 apple, cored, and chopped (you don't have to peel it)

3 cups chicken broth

2 $\frac{1}{2}$ to 3 lb boneless turkey breast, mostly thawed by putting in the refrigerator overnight or in the microwave, follow directions (find in frozen poultry section of grocery store)

1 tsp salt

$\frac{1}{2}$ tsp pepper

DIRECTIONS

Mix together the rice, onion, dried cranberries, apple, and rice seasoning packets.

Place in bottom of Crock-Pot.

Pour broth over, making sure all rice is covered. Add extra water if necessary.

Season turkey with salt and pepper and place on top of rice mixture.

Cook on Low for 8 hours until turkey is thoroughly cooked and rice is tender.

Serves 6

Warm Chocolate Mess

This recipe tastes just like the dessert called "Chocolate Stuff" that my nephew loves from a restaurant in St. Simon's on the Georgia coast. The chocolate chips take it over the top. Good with vanilla, cherry, or peppermint ice cream. Just plain good!

INGREDIENTS

1 pkg. chocolate cake mix

3 oz pkg instant chocolate pudding mix

4 eggs

1 cup water

2 cups sour cream (16 oz container)

¾ cup vegetable oil

¼ tsp salt

1 cup semisweet chocolate chips

DIRECTIONS

Spray Crock-Pot with cooking spray.

In a large bowl, combine eggs with the water, then add the sour cream and oil and stir until smooth.

Add the dry ingredients and beat well.

Stir in the chocolate chips.

Pour into Crock-Pot.

Cover and cook on Low for 4 to 5 hours, until top springs back when touched very lightly with a finger.

Serves 8 to 10 or one nephew

Suggestion: Store leftovers in the refrigerator and microwave to reheat.

Substantial Sides

In a world of fast-food, takeout, and commercially prepared convenience foods, the simple side dish has sort of fallen out of favor. I say we bring the side dish back with these delicious recipes. Some of the more substantial ones, like Mama's Mac 'n Cheese, page 120, can sneak over to the entrée side of the dinner plate. The Baked Potato Bar, page 117, is a great and inexpensive way to throw a party. Pesto for Pasta, page 121, can also be a lovely summer supper.

The truth is, many home cooks rely on casseroles and one-pot main dishes that require only a salad to elevate them to a complete and satisfying meal.

Still, there are times when you need a perfect side dish to round out your menu. I wouldn't think of serving a meatloaf without the Potatoes au Gratin, page 122. They go together like an old married couple. Who eats a burger without fries? The Sweet Potato Fries, page 127, are so easy to make, and are actually quite healthy.

The truth is, many sides are so simple that you don't need much of a recipe. Dropping some broccoli in boiling water for three minutes, then draining it and adding a little butter or cheese isn't rocket science. Hit the grocery store salad bar and you have everything you need for a quick stir-fry. Several of these recipes work perfectly when you want something interesting and tasty to go with a simple sautéed chicken breast or a broiled steak. These recipes are all easy to prepare and will add that special little something to any meal.

Here are some ideas for quick sides for those occasions when you have no prep time:

Spinach Sauté

Sauté prewashed, bagged spinach in olive oil and sliced garlic until wilted, 2 to 3 minutes. Add salt and pepper and nutmeg if you have any.

Stuffed Tomatoes

Cut the tops off tomatoes and scoop out seeds. Fill with seasoned breadcrumbs, or crumbled salad croutons plus a sprinkle of Parmesan cheese and bake at 350 for 30 minutes.

Roasted Root Vegetables

Crank up your oven to 450 degrees. On a baking sheet lined with foil, place root vegetables coated in olive oil, salt, and pepper. Roast until tender, usually 20 to 30 minutes. A favorite combination is cubed potatoes, quartered onions, and carrots cut in chunks. Other choices include turnips, parsnips, sweet potatoes, and beets.

Roasted Broccoli, Asparagus, or Green Beans

Follow the method for Roasted Root Vegetables and shorten the cooking time to about 10 minutes. A sprinkle of fresh grated Parmesan cheese for the last minute of cooking time is another way to get great flavor.

Microwave Steaming

Use the microwave to steam tender, quick cooking-vegetables, like asparagus, green beans, or zucchini. Just put them in a microwave-safe dish with a little water and a damp paper towel on top. Steam for 3 minutes and then check for doneness. Add salt and pepper and maybe a squeeze of lemon juice. I love to stir in leftover Tomato Topping, page 16.

Baked Potato Bar

(Also great for dinner or appetizers)

INGREDIENTS

Baking potatoes, one for each person

POSSIBLE TOPPINGS

Butter

Sour cream

Grated cheese, any kind you like

Bacon or bacon bits

Green onions, sliced

Leftover proteins—steak, chicken, salmon, or shrimp

Chili, homemade or canned

Cooked vegetables like broccoli, mushrooms, red pepper (grocery store salad bar)

Pizza sauce

Ranch dressing

Salsa

Cooked sausage

Cubed ham or turkey

Pepperoni

Caviar, affordable if you get small jars found with canned seafood

Smoked oysters

DIRECTIONS

Rinse and scrub potatoes to get off any dirt. Bake at 400 degrees for an hour.

To Serve: Put potatoes on a serving tray. You can leave them whole or slice open the top. Put your choices of toppings in bowls and let guests create their own potato. I always include butter and sour cream and then pick 4 or 5 toppings from the list. Use your grocery store salad bar.

Serving Suggestion: You can use small new potatoes and make this an appetizer. Put the potatoes on a foil-lined baking sheet, toss with a little olive oil, and sprinkle with a little salt before baking. Bake for 30 minutes and check one for doneness. Serve as a mini baked potato bar with toppings of choice. Scoop out the very top with a small spoon before serving if desired for a nice presentation.

Fresh Squash Casserole

One of my neighbors had an impressive squash crop last summer and brought this dish to a potluck supper. I couldn't get enough of it, and fortunately she shared her recipe. The chiles make it a little different, and I appreciate the fact that it contains no breadcrumbs or gloppy yellow-cheese product! This is a recipe that will convert even the most determined squash hater. Yum.

INGREDIENTS

6 medium to large yellow squash, sliced in 1-inch rounds

½ onion, chopped

2 tbsp butter

4 oz cream cheese

4 oz can chopped green chiles

1 tsp salt

1 tbsp sugar

1 egg

Optional: paprika for topping

DIRECTIONS

Preheat oven to 350 degrees.

Put the squash and onion in a large saucepan and add water to just cover.

Boil for 15 to 20 minutes until tender.

Drain very well in a colander to make sure your casserole won't be watery.

Return squash to the same pan and mash up a little bit with a potato masher or a fork.

Add remaining ingredients to squash and onions, except egg, and mix well.

Beat the egg in a small bowl. Add to squash mixture, stirring to combine.

Pour mixture into an 8 × 8 baking dish, or similar size casserole dish, sprayed with cooking spray.

Sprinkle with paprika if desired.

Bake for 30 minutes until set.

Serves 6

Green Beans Everyone Likes!

Green beans can seem like a boring vegetable because they are available and affordable all year long. That means they have become the universal side dish. This recipe knocks boredom out of the window.

INGREDIENTS

1 lb green beans (if they have a stems, pop them off)

½ tsp salt

2 tsp sesame oil

1 tbsp sesame seeds

¼ tsp salt (coarse sea salt is best here for some crunch, but not essential)

DIRECTIONS

Put green beans in a microwave-safe dish, add ½ cup of water and salt, and cover with plastic wrap. Microwave for 5 minutes.

Carefully pull back plastic wrap and test one bean to see if it is tender, but still a little crisp. Microwave a minute more if necessary.

Drain and rinse with cold water. (The cold-water rinse helps the beans stay bright green.)

Pat green beans with a paper towel to remove most of the water.

Put green beans in a serving dish and toss with sesame seeds, sesame oil, and salt to taste.

These are delicious warm or at room temperature.

Leftover green beans will keep for 2 days in the refrigerator.

Serves 4

Mama's Mac 'n Cheese

Macaroni and cheese is the ultimate comfort food. My son quickly discovered that those little boxes and microwavable containers are no substitute for the real deal. This recipe is for a baked macaroni and cheese, which is very much a Southern specialty. Sure, you could eat the whole thing right out of the pot without baking it, but it's awfully attractive bubbling hot and lightly browned in a casserole dish. The breadcrumbs are optional for a little crunch on top. I know this is technically a side dish, but I would eat Mac 'n Cheese for a dinner entrée anytime and not complain a bit!

INGREDIENTS

1 box pasta shells or elbows

6 tbsp butter

6 tbsp flour

2½ cups milk

1 tsp salt

½ tsp pepper

8 oz grated sharp cheddar cheese—or experiment with a combination, such as Swiss, Gruyere, or Jarlsberg (reserve ¼ cup for topping)

Optional: ⅛ tsp nutmeg

Optional: topping of 2 pieces of toasted bread, crumbled, mixed with 1 tbsp melted butter (*hint: Melt butter in the microwave in a small cup or bowl.*)

DIRECTIONS

Preheat oven to 350 degrees.

Cook pasta according to the package directions. Drain.

Melt the butter in a large saucepan, over medium heat.

Whisk in flour and cook for 1 minute.

Gradually add milk and cook until thick. (*hint: If the sauce seems too thick add ¼ cup more milk.*)

Stir in cheese, reserving ¼ cup to sprinkle over the top.

Add nutmeg to the sauce if you are using it.

Spray a large baking dish with cooking spray.

Mix sauce with pasta and pour in baking dish.

Top with reserved cheese and breadcrumbs, if desired.

Bake for about 20 minutes until hot and bubbly.

Serves 8

Pesto for Pasta, Vegetables, etc.

If you make this pesto, you have the possibility for so many dishes. Of course, it is great on hot pasta, but consider pesto as a dressing for sliced tomatoes and onions, serve it with raw veggies as a dip, spread it on toasted baguettes, use it in a pasta salad, top hot grilled fish or chicken with it—the possibilities are endless.

INGREDIENTS

2 cups basil leaves *(hint: If it isn't summer and basil is expensive, substitute half of the basil with spinach)*

¼ cup toasted walnuts or pine nuts (pine nuts can be expensive)

⅓ cup Parmesan cheese, grated

½ tsp salt

¼ to ½ cup olive oil

For serving: hot pasta, or any ingredients for the dishes suggested at the top of the page

DIRECTIONS

Mix all ingredients in a blender or food processor. Start by including ¼ cup olive oil and add more as needed to get a thick paste that isn't too dry.

Stir into hot pasta, or use in any of the ways mentioned above.

Makes about 1 ½ cups

Suggestion: Leftover pesto will keep for several days with a thin layer of olive oil on top in a covered container in the fridge.

You can also freeze pesto in ice trays to add to sauces. Freeze and then put cubes in a Baggie. Use in pasta sauce or soup in place of dried basil.

Potatoes au Gratin

INGREDIENTS

3 potatoes, sliced into ¼-inch thick slices (no need to peel)

1 onion, sliced into rings

2 tsp salt to sprinkle layers

1 tsp pepper to sprinkle layers

3 tbsp butter

3 tbsp flour

2 cups milk

½ tsp salt

1½ cups grated cheddar cheese

DIRECTIONS

Preheat oven to 400 degrees.

Spray a 9 × 13 casserole with cooking spray.

Layer half of the potatoes in the casserole.

Sprinkle with 1 tsp salt and ½ tsp pepper.

Top with the onion slices, and add the remaining potatoes.

Sprinkle with 1 tsp salt and ½ tsp pepper.

In a medium saucepan, melt butter over medium heat.

Mix in the flour and stir constantly for one minute.

Stir in milk and ½ tsp salt. Cook until mixture has thickened.

Add cheese all at once, and stir until melted, 1 minute.

Pour cheese mixture over the potatoes, and cover the dish with aluminum foil.

Bake 1½ hours.

Remove from oven and change oven setting to broil.

Uncover casserole and broil for 1 or 2 minutes to lightly brown the top, watching to make sure it doesn't get too brown.

Serves 6

Serving Suggestion: This is a great cheese sauce. You can pour it over toast for a quick version of Welsh Rarebit.

Roasted Vegetables with Rice

INGREDIENTS

1 head of broccoli, including the stem, cut in bite-sized pieces

1 onion, diced

1 red, green, or yellow bell pepper, diced

2 tbsp olive oil

1 tsp salt

½ tsp pepper

1 package wild and long rice mix

Optional: ¼ cup chopped roasted salted almonds or slivered almonds

DIRECTIONS

Preheat oven to 450 degrees.

Line a baking sheet with aluminum foil and add vegetables in a single layer.

Toss the vegetables with oil, salt, and pepper and bake at 450 degrees for 20 minutes.

Stir and bake 10 more minutes.

Cook rice according to package directions.

Mix hot rice and vegetables and sprinkle almonds on top.

Serves 4

Suggestion: You could definitely use other vegetables like yellow squash or zucchini.

Serving Suggestion: A sprinkle of Parmesan over the top is a nice extra touch.

Spaghetti Squash

When spaghetti squash is cooked, it looks exactly like angel-hair pasta. It has about 30 calories a cup—if you're counting. The flavor is wonderful and the "noodles" can handle almost any sauce. What a perfect vegetable!

INGREDIENTS

1 spaghetti squash

Water

1 tsp salt

Toppings of choice: butter, Parmesan cheese, ricotta cheese, sautéed garlic, tomato sauce, pesto sauce, fresh herbs

DIRECTIONS

Cut squash in half long ways and scoop out seeds.

Place face down in a glass dish that will fit in your microwave. You may need to cook each half separately. *see note

Add water to the depth of 1 inch and add 1 tsp of salt.

Cover with plastic wrap and microwave for 10 minutes.

Carefully remove plastic wrap, turn squash over, and scoop out the strands with a fork.

Add toppings you like. Butter and Parmesan cheese with a grind of pepper are hard to beat.

1 squash makes a side dish for 2 to 3 people

*Spaghetti squash can also be baked in the oven, cut-side down in water. It takes about 45 minutes in a 350 degree oven.

Stir-Fry Rice

INGREDIENTS

4 cups cooked white rice (2 cups dry rice cooked in 4 cups water, follow package directions) *see note

2 eggs

2 tsp sesame oil, divided, half to cook egg, half to drizzle over rice

⅓ cup shredded carrots (grocery store salad bar)

⅓ cup green sliced green onions (grocery store salad bar)

½ cup frozen green peas

2 tbsp vegetable oil

Optional: red pepper flakes for topping

2 tsp soy

DIRECTIONS

Whisk eggs in a small bowl.

In a large nonstick skillet, heat 1 tsp sesame oil.

Pour in eggs and move skillet around to let eggs spread to a thin layer.

Cook about a minute and flip.

Remove to a plate and slice in strips.

Heat 1 tbsp vegetable oil in same skillet, and sauté carrots and onions about 3 minutes.

Remove to plate with eggs.

Add 1 tbsp vegetable oil to skillet and add rice. Fry one minute.

Add peas and soy sauce, and toss rice to coat.

Add eggs, and vegetables.

Drizzle with sesame oil, add red pepper flakes if using, and toss again.

Serves 4

*If you have time, cook rice ahead of time and let it cool in the refrigerator. It fries better.

Serving Suggestion: If you add cooked chicken, beef, shrimp, or pork, it's a delicious main dish for 2.

Sweet Potato Fries

INGREDIENTS

2 sweet potatoes, peeled and cut lengthwise in ¼-inch-thick fries

2 tbsp olive oil

1 tsp each, salt, paprika and pepper, or to taste (you can experiment with other seasonings, like Old Bay or Montreal Steak Seasoning)

DIRECTIONS

Preheat oven to 450 degrees.

Put potatoes in a medium bowl with oil and seasoning and toss to coat.

Line a baking sheet with parchment paper or aluminum foil. *(hint: The parchment paper is great to use because nothing sticks to it. Find it with foil and Baggies.)*

Spread potatoes in pan so they aren't touching and bake for about 20 minutes, turning once.

Serves 4

Serving Suggestion: Make your fries special with a unique and delicious ketchup. Combine ¼ cup ketchup and ¼ cup barbeque sauce or go for another flavor with ¼ cup ketchup and ¼ cup salsa. Yum!

INTRODUCTION TO

Bread and Breakfast

Let's be honest—when you are running out the door at 7:30 in the morning and possibly late for school, work, or whatever your day may hold, cooking breakfast is not a reasonable proposition. I do believe in breakfast and rely on cereal, quick-cooked eggs and toast, instant oatmeal, fruit and cottage cheese, yogurt, and frequently, leftovers—microwaved or not.

Breakfast really is a favorite meal for so many people. In my perfect life I would have a delicious breakfast everyday. Since that's not possible, I make up for it on weekends, vacations, and holidays. On weekday evenings we sometime splurge with our favorite little dinner we call "Brenner"—breakfast for dinner. For a busy person, a weekend brunch is a fantastic and economical way to entertain. First of all eggs are the cheapest thing in the world, and omelets are the most delicious. A Make Your Own Omelet Party, recipe for Cheese Omelet, page 137, for four or five of your favorite people is simple to pull off with a few grocery store salad bar toppings like peppers, onions, and mushrooms, and a bag of shredded cheese. You could go all out and cook some sausage if the mood is right!

Make the recipe for Favorite Coffee Cake, page 140, brew a pot of coffee, and friends will just show up at your door. It smells that great. If you are grown enough to actually be twenty-one or older, stir up some mimosas with lots of orange juice and a bit of champagne. Then, make a batch of Beignets at Home, page 132, for a really fabulous brunch.

The bread recipes in this section are just a delight. They make a perfect contribution to a potluck, a beautiful hostess gift, and for me, baking is a way to unwind. It's easy to fall in love with baking bread. A bonus of course, is that your home smells heavenly. Here's a clever trick—soften butter or cream cheese enough to mix in honey or your favorite jam or jelly and you have a flavored spread to serve with your bread. Try cream cheese and strawberry jam with the Strawberry Bread, page 143. You won't

Almost *Red Lobster* Biscuits

My sister wanted me to change the name of these biscuits because she couldn't find any lobster in the ingredients list. I wouldn't dare change it because if you've ever been to a Red Lobster restaurant you know how addictive the biscuits are. These taste just like the real thing! They're definitely man-catching biscuits—I've never met a guy who isn't crazy for them. But if you're a guy, it probably works both ways. Try these and find out.

INGREDIENTS

2½ cups Bisquick

¾ cup milk

½ stick butter, softened (5 to 6 seconds in the microwave)

½ tsp garlic salt or powder

1 cup grated cheddar cheese

FOR TOP

2 tbsp butter

½ tsp garlic salt

Optional: dried parsley for sprinkling is just for looks *(hint: The garlic salt I buy has dried parsley in it already.)*

DIRECTIONS

Preheat oven to 400 degrees.

In a large bowl, mix Bisquick, butter, garlic salt, and cheese.

Add milk until combined. Don't over mix or the biscuits will be tough.

Drop spoonfuls onto an ungreased baking sheet.

Bake for 15 to 17 minutes until tops are brown.

Melt butter in the microwave in a small bowl and stir in garlic salt.

Brush biscuits with butter mixture. *(hint: If you don't have a pastry brush, use a spoon to lightly drizzle the butter over the biscuits.)*

Makes 12 to 15

Beignets at Home

Channeling Gertrude Stein, I like to say, "Nashville is my city, but New Orleans is my other hometown." I love it there; New Orleans is hands down my favorite destination. It's partly the food, of course, and partly the culture, and mostly the magic. Speaking of magic, I once went to a convention in New Orleans with my husband, and there were a series of activities for spouses. Weirdly, I was the only person who selected, "How to Use Voodoo Effectively," so I had my own private lessons and never looked back. Many times I have been able to say, "I have a voodoo doll, and I know how to use it!" Handy!

In no way are these beignets as delicious as Café Du Monde's—nothing is, but they're yummy all the same and just a cinch to prepare. We make them all the time.

INGREDIENTS

1 roll of crescent dough

2 cups canola oil

½ cup confectioners' sugar

DIRECTIONS

Heat oil in a medium-sized saucepan over medium-high heat.

Unroll dough and cut each crescent into three pieces, they don't all have to be the exact same shape and size, for 24 total pieces.

Drop in hot oil, three at a time, and let fry quickly, turning to make sure both sides are a light golden brown. *(hint: Drop a small piece of dough into the hot oil to see if it is ready. You don't want the oil to smoke or it's too hot.)*

It takes less than a minute for each batch to cook.

Drain on paper towels and roll in confectioners' sugar.

Serves 4

Delicious served with hot coffee mixed with hot milk. Chicory coffee blend is traditional and can be found in many grocery stores.

Buttermilk Biscuits

INGREDIENTS

2 cups self-rising flour *see note

1 tsp sugar

½ stick cold butter, cut in small pieces

¾ cup buttermilk **see note

DIRECTIONS

Preheat oven to 425 degrees.

In a large mixing bowl or in a food processor, combine flour, sugar and butter. (hint: Mixing by hand will yield flakier biscuits.)

Add buttermilk until just blended.

On a floured work area, roll or pat out dough about 1-inch thick. (hint: Use wax paper on your counter with a little flour on it.)

Cut with a biscuit cutter or a drinking glass. Reroll and cut scraps.

Put on an ungreased baking sheet. (hint: I bake mine packed closely together in my cast iron skillet.)

Bake for 12 to 15 minutes until lightly browned. (hint: A famous TV chef beat out our much missed local "biscuit lady" with a similar recipe by brushing the top of the biscuits with cream and sprinkling with pepper before baking.)

Makes 12 to 14

* To make self-rising flour, mix 2 cups flour with 1 tbsp baking powder and 1 tsp salt.

**If you don't have buttermilk, mix a tablespoon of vinegar or lemon juice in a cup of regular milk, let it sit a minute, and use in recipe.

Bonus Recipe: Cream Gravy

Melt 2 tbsp butter in a small saucepan. Whisk in 2 tbsp flour. Cook, stirring constantly for 1 minute. Whisk in 1½ cups of milk. Continue to stir until thick. Season to taste with salt and pepper. If you want sausage gravy, add about ½ cup cooked, crumbled breakfast sausage. Serve with biscuits.

Buttermilk Pancakes, with Easy, No Mess Baked Bacon, p. 139

Buttermilk Pancakes

I'll never understand why people wait in long lines all morning at restaurants with goofy names for a pancake. Come on! Pancakes are the easiest thing in the world to prepare and about impossible to mess up. Yes, pancakes are delicious, but don't you have better things to do with your time than wait in a line for them? Make your own, and enjoy the superior taste of homemade pancakes plus all that extra naptime! My son adds chocolate chips; I like blueberries.

INGREDIENTS

2 cups self-rising flour *see note

2 tbsp sugar

2 cups buttermilk **see note

4 tbsp melted butter *(hint: Melt in the microwave in a small cup or bowl.)*

2 eggs

Extra butter for cooking or cooking spray

DIRECTIONS

Mix all ingredients for pancakes.

Heat a skillet over medium-high heat.

Add a 1 tsp of butter or spray with cooking spray. *(hint: Butter makes the pancakes have those pretty little brown edges.)*

Pour a large spoonful of batter in the skillet for each pancake. Make 2 or 3 at a time. Add more butter for each batch.

Cook until little bubbles start to form, then flip.

Cook until lightly browned on both sides.

(hint: Keep the pancakes warm in a 200-degree oven while you get them all cooked.)

Serve with butter and syrup. Please use real maple syrup. The imitation maple syrup is just hideous.

Serves 4

* To make self-rising flour, mix 2 cups flour with 1 tbsp baking powder and 1 tsp salt.

** If you don't have buttermilk, mix a tablespoon of vinegar or lemon juice in a cup of regular milk, let it sit a minute, and use in recipe.

Cheese Omelet

The first time I went to New York, I was twenty-two years old. My cousin took me to an omelet restaurant where the claim to fame was having a thousand omelets on the menu. Little did he know I would insist on reading the whole thing. (I love a good menu.) It was also the first of many sticker shocks I had on that trip, but come on, sixteen dollars for an omelet, no bacon included, was and is highway robbery!

According to legend, or fact, as the town of Bessières, France, would have you believe, The Giant Easter Omelet came to be when Napoleon stopped in the town for the night. The story goes that Napoleon feasted on an omelet prepared by a local innkeeper. The dish was such a culinary delight that he ordered the towns-people to gather all the eggs in the village and prepare a huge omelet for his army the next day. That sounds like a lot of trouble.

Here is the recipe that Richard likes and asked me to put in the cookbook. If you add spinach and mush-rooms, you could probably sell your omelet for thirty dollars today in New York!

INGREDIENTS

2 eggs

1 tbsp water

¼ tsp each, salt and pepper

2 tsp butter

⅓ cup of your favorite cheese

DIRECTIONS

In a small bowl beat eggs with water, salt, and pepper until very well blended. A fork or a whisk will do the trick.

Melt butter in an 8-inch nonstick skillet over medium heat.

Tilt the skillet to coat the bottom.

Pour in the egg mixture. It should start to set right away.

With a spatula, push edges of omelet to the center of skillet and let raw egg slide on to the skillet sur-face.

When the surface of the eggs is thick and no raw egg remains, place cheese on one side of the omelet and fold the other side over with a spatula.

Slide onto a plate and enjoy!

Serves 1

Serving Suggestion: So many things make good omelet fillings: salsa, ham, cooked spinach, cooked mushrooms, peppers, onions, and tomatoes to name a few! (grocery store salad bar)

Easiest Rolls

Once in college, I went to a dinner party and we were served these rolls along with cauliflower soup. The soup was weird, bordering on disgusting, but the rolls saved the day. I thought maybe I liked them so much because of the horrible soup, but when I found myself craving them a few days later I called the host and got the recipe. (He also gave me the soup recipe, and I bet you know what happened to that.) I made the rolls immediately and discovered they really are delicious.

INGREDIENTS

1 cup self-rising flour *see note

½ cup milk

1 tsp sugar

2 tbsp mayonnaise (really, it works great)

DIRECTIONS

Preheat oven to 350 degrees.

Mix all ingredients.

Pour into muffin tins sprayed with cooking spray and bake for 15 minutes.

Makes 6 regular size rolls

*To make self-rising flour, mix 2 cups flour with 1 tbsp baking powder, and 1 tsp salt.

Suggestion: Want to dress them up? Sprinkle with sesame or poppy seeds before baking.

Easy, No-Mess Baked Bacon

I cannot believe how brilliant this is for serving a crowd. We frequently vacation with a family who likes bacon as much as we do, and this beats the heck out of frying up numerous pans of the stuff. It's great for a small number too—no splattering grease, easy cleanup—what's not to like? Try the syrup or brown-sugar idea, but watch out—it's addictive.

INGREDIENTS

Bacon—thin sliced cooks faster than thick sliced

DIRECTIONS

Preheat oven to 400 degrees.

Line a baking sheet with foil. If you crinkle the foil up a little the bacon can drain better—just make sure the whole pan is covered.

Alternately, if you have a baking rack that fits your pan, you can use that. You should still line the pan with foil for easier cleanup.

Lay bacon slices in prepared pan leaving about 1 inch between slices.

Bake for 14 to 18 minutes, checking occasionally for doneness.

If you like bacon extra crunchy, bake a little longer checking frequently.

Drain on paper towels.

2 to 3 slices per person

Suggestion: For a special treat, I like to brush a tiny bit of maple syrup on each piece. You have to check that it doesn't brown too quickly. Alternately, you can sprinkle on a little brown sugar about half-way through cooking.

Favorite Coffee Cake

I was proudly showing off the rough draft of this cookbook to a college-aged friend of mine. She was thumbing through, and when she got to this recipe, she whipped out her phone to take a picture of it! I promised I'd e-mail the recipe ASAP, but hey, a picture's worth a thousand e-mails.

INGREDIENTS

Cake

2 cups Bisquick

2 tbsp sugar

1 egg

⅔ cup milk

TOPPING

⅓ cup Bisquick

⅓ cup brown sugar

½ tsp cinnamon

3 tbsp butter (not melted)

DIRECTIONS

Preheat oven to 400 degrees.

Mix all ingredients for cake in a medium bowl.

Mix topping ingredients in a small bowl with a fork until crumbly.

Spray a pie pan or 8 × 8 baking dish with cooking spray.

Pour in batter and sprinkle topping over it.

Bake for 25 minutes.

Serves 6

French Toast

Picture on page 128.

INGREDIENTS

3 eggs

⅓ cup milk

1 tsp vanilla

⅛ tsp nutmeg

2 tbsp butter for cooking

8 pieces of 1-inch thick bread, Texas toast, or French bread *see note

TOPPING POSSIBILITIES:

sliced strawberries or other berries (grocery store salad bar)

confectioners' sugar

maple syrup (don't buy the imitation maple syrup; it's disgusting)

butter

DIRECTIONS

Beat eggs, milk, vanilla, and nutmeg in a shallow dish wide enough to hold a bread slice.

Heat a large skillet over medium-high heat. Add ½ tbsp of the butter to melt.

Dip 2 bread slices in egg mixture, turning to soak both sides.

Cook in the skillet on both sides until lightly browned, one to two minutes per side.

Repeat with remaining bread slices.

(hint: Keep warm in a 200-degree oven while you cook the rest.)

Serves 4

*To make for one person, use 2 pieces of bread, 1 egg, 3 tbsp milk, and ⅓ tsp vanilla.

Suggestion: This is great with Easy, No-Mess Baked Bacon, page 139. If you start the bacon first, you have time to get the French toast done to serve with perfectly crispy bacon.

Scones the Way You Like Them

Who says you have to follow the rules? This recipe might make a British person go crazy (currants only, please), but I'm not a British person, and I like to play around with the taste and texture of these scones. Lately I've had a thing for dried cranberries and walnuts in my scones. See what you can invent!

INGREDIENTS

2 cups flour

⅓ cup brown sugar

1 tbsp baking powder

1 tsp salt

1 stick butter

½ cup half & half or milk

1 egg

YOUR CHOICE OF INGREDIENTS

1 cup of any of these: dried berries, raisins, or chopped fruit; coconut; nuts; chocolate; white chocolate; or butterscotch chips. You could definitely do a mix.

DIRECTIONS

Preheat oven to 400 degrees.

Mix dry ingredients in a large bowl.

Cut the stick of butter in little pieces and work into flour mixture with your hands or use 2 forks. If you have a food processor you can mix up the dough in it. *(hint: Mixing by hand yields flakier scones.)*

Mix egg and half & half together and add to dough until just blended. If you over mix, the scones will be tough.

Stir in ingredient(s) of choice.

Drop by spoonfuls onto a baking sheet sprayed with cooking spray.

Bake for 18 to 20 minutes until golden brown.

Serve with butter, or just eat them plain; they're delicious!

Makes about 12

Strawberry Bread

I love, love, love this recipe. It's the perfect gift for a friend or hostess. This can make you forget a bad day.

INGREDIENTS

8 oz pkg frozen strawberries, thawed; or 1 cup fresh strawberries, sliced

1½ cups flour

1 cup sugar

1 tsp cinnamon

½ tsp salt

½ tsp baking soda

½ cup vegetable oil

2 eggs, beaten

Optional: ½ cup chopped pecans

DIRECTIONS

Preheat oven to 350 degrees.

Butter and flour a 9 × 5 loaf pan, or spray with baking spray.

Put strawberries in medium-sized bowl.

Combine flour, sugar, cinnamon, salt, and baking soda in large bowl and mix well.

Blend oil and eggs into strawberries.

Add strawberry mixture to flour mixture, stirring until dry ingredients are just moistened.

Stir in pecans.

Pour the batter into the prepared pan.

Bake for 50 to 60 minutes until the center is done.

Let cool in pan for 10 minutes.

Turn loaf out, and cool completely. (Ha! That never happens here.)

Makes 1 loaf

Haystacks, p. 154; Super Easy Fudge, p. 163; No Cook Apricot and Coconut Cookies, p. 156

INTRODUCTION TO
Desserts

I don't care what anybody says, dessert is what we're all waiting for! Whether it is a plate of yummy cookies or a fancy but easy to make Pot de Crème, page 161, a little sweet bite is always the star of the show. Some of these are so simple they can be a last-minute thought. Who doesn't want a two-minute Instant Microwave Chocolate Cake, page 155, in a coffee cup? Just delicious! The Saltine Cookies, page 162, are a sweet surprise and take no time to make, just like the Haystacks, page 154.

Desserts are also wonderful to share. The blender Chocolate and Caramel sauces, pages 148, are perfect hostess gifts to take when you're invited to dinner at a significant other's parent's home. They're both also wonderful to keep around and use as an ice cream topping or a dip for fresh fruit. Make a nice container of Fudge Brownies, page 151, to either bribe a surly boss or perk up a down-and-out friend.

One of my all-time favorite desserts is Peach Mountain Rollups, page 158. Even if everyone at the table says they're too full for dessert, when you take this out of the oven they will devour it. I recently served this after a huge multi-course Italian meal and found the pan completely empty at the end of the night. It's also true that my own family thinks I've let them down terribly if there is no Fudge Pie, page 152, in the house. It's considered a staple like milk and peanut butter. It's fun to make the No Bake Apricot and Coconut Cookies, page 156, and keep them in the fridge for late-night snacking. For a party serve One of Everything Fruit Pie Crumble, page 157. It's got that kind of old-fashioned goodness that tastes like you've spent all day in the kitchen!

Whether you're a chocoholic or just want a tiny sweet bite at the end of the night, you will find so many things to love here. If you're feeling a little adventurous remember that the Crock-Pot/slow cooker section has a couple of delicious desserts to try.

Banana Cream Pie

INGREDIENTS

1 refrigerated piecrust (*hint: It's fine to get the frozen ones in aluminum pans, but the piecrusts that you unroll and place in the pan are better and no more trouble if you own a pie pan. Find them with biscuits and cookie dough in the grocery store. Or make your own, page 63.*)

3.4 oz pkg instant vanilla pudding and pie filling

2 cups milk

2 to 3 ripe bananas, sliced into ¼-inch rounds

1 cup whipped cream, **bonus recipe**, page 147 (*hint: Frozen whipped topping is disgusting. Whipped cream in a can is actu-ally made with cream and tastes okay. It goes flat after a day.*)

Optional: chocolate shavings for garnish *see note

DIRECTIONS

Preheat oven to 350 degrees.

Put pudding mix in a large bowl, add 2 cups cold milk, and whisk for 2 minutes. Refrigerate to thicken until ready to use.

Place the piecrust in a pie pan and prick the dough several times with a fork.

Bake piecrust 15 minutes, checking to make sure it doesn't get too brown.

Let crust cool.

Line the bottom of the piecrust with the bananas. Spoon the pudding over the bananas and smooth to cover. Spread a layer of the whipped cream on top, and garnish with the chocolate shavings.

Serve immediately or refrigerate.

Serves 6

*To make chocolate shavings, use a vegetable peeler, or, if you don't have one, use a small sharp knife. Shave off pieces of your favorite chocolate candy bar.

Bonus Recipe: Whipped Cream

This recipe works best if you put the cream, the bowl, and the beaters in the freezer for 10 minutes before you start. Pour 1 cup of cream in a bowl - glass or metal are best, but use what you have. Beat with an electric mixer at high speed adding ¼ cup sugar until stiff peaks form. That's it—you have whipped cream.

You can actually make this in your blender as well. Just blend until thick.

(hint: I see hand-held electric beaters at flea markets and Goodwill all the time.)

Caramel Sauce in the Blender

INGREDIENTS

$^2/_3$ cup brown sugar

2 tbsp butter

$^1/_4$ tsp salt

$^1/_2$ cup hot evaporated milk *(hint: Heat in the microwave in a small bowl, but don't boil.)*

DIRECTIONS

Put all ingredients in blender and blend until combined. Cool and store in a jar in the refrigerator. Reheat in microwave. Keeps for a month.

Makes about 1 $^1/_2$ cups

Chocolate Sauce in the Blender

INGREDIENTS

1 tbsp butter

$^1/_2$ lb semisweet chocolate chips

1 cup hot cream *(hint: Heat in the microwave in a small bowl, but don't boil.)*

DIRECTIONS

Put all ingredients in blender and blend until combined. Cool and store in a jar in the refrigerator. Reheat in microwave. Keeps for a month.

Makes about 1 $^1/_2$ cups

Both sauces are delicious on ice cream or cake.

Suggestion: Both of these make a great hostess gift or Christmas present. Print gift labels on your computer, describing what this gift is and how long it will keep in the refrigerator. You'll definitely make friends with these treats.!

Dessert Pizza Cookie

This cookie makes an adorable birthday present. To give this as a gift or take it to a party, see if you can beg or buy an unused pizza box from a local pizza restaurant and serve it from the box. Children and grown-ups go crazy over this.

INGREDIENTS

Flour for work surface *(hint: I use wax paper with a little flour on it on my counter as a work space.)*

1 tube refrigerated sugar cookie dough

1 cup M&M'S *see note

½ cup chopped Snickers bars

⅓ cup mini-marshmallows

DIRECTIONS

Preheat oven to 350 degrees.

On a lightly floured surface, roll the cookie dough into a ball.

Transfer the ball to a baking sheet sprayed with cooking spray, or a pizza pan if you have one, and roll into a 12-inch circle, flouring the rolling pin as needed.

Bake 12 to 15 minutes.

Remove from oven and top with M&M'S, Snickers, and marshmallows.

Return to the oven and bake for another 7 minutes, to soften candies.

To serve, cut cookie into wedges.

Serves 6 to 8

*You can make this seasonal by using M&M'S that are produced in different colors for holidays: orange and black for Halloween, red and green for Christmas, pink for Valentine's Day, pastels for Easter, and red, white, and blue for the Fourth of July.

Frozen No-Bake Key Lime Pie

INGREDIENTS

½ cup Key lime juice (with fruit juices and sometimes with cocktail mixers at the grocery store)

Zest and juice of 1 lime *(hint: Use a cheese grater to grate zest.)* *see note

½ box of lime Jell-O

1 can sweetened condensed milk (find this in the baking section)

4 oz (half a tub) frozen whipped topping, (okay, this is one time you can use it; the pie is frozen so the texture won't matter as much)

1 graham-cracker piecrust (in the baking section)

DIRECTIONS

Put juice and zest in a bowl.

Whisk in Jell-O until it dissolves; it takes about a minute.

Stir in condensed milk, then whisk in whipped topping.

Pour in crust and freeze.

Takes 4 to 6 hours to freeze.

Serves 6 to 8

Suggestion: Easy to double because you have ½ of a package of Jell-O and ½ of a tub of whipped topping left over—you would need to buy 1 extra lime, 1 extra can of condensed milk, and another piecrust. Since you freeze the dessert, it keeps for a while.

Suggestion: If you want to make this very diet friendly, use fat-free condensed milk, sugar-free Jell-O, and fat-free whipped topping. Sometimes it pays to have a low-calorie treat to fall back on.

*Zest is the grated outside peel. Don't use the white part of a citrus fruit.

Fudge Brownies

INGREDIENTS

1 stick butter

5 tbsp unsweetened cocoa powder

1 cup sugar

2 eggs

1 tsp vanilla

¾ cup flour

DIRECTIONS

Preheat oven to 350 degrees.

Melt butter in the microwave in a medium bowl and add cocoa powder.

Stir in sugar and add eggs and vanilla.

Stir in flour and mix well.

Spread in an 8 × 8 baking dish sprayed with cooking spray.

Bake for 25 to 30 minutes.

Cool and cut into equal pieces.

Makes 12

Suggestion: This is a very basic but delicious recipe. You can add ingredients for interesting flavors like 1 tsp of instant coffee, ½ cup of nuts, mini-marshmallows, or toffee bits. Add a sprinkle of cayenne pepper and cinnamon and you've got **"hot chocolate"** brownies. The possibilities are endless.

Fudge Pie

This pie has always been the gold standard in our house. My mom made it without a crust and is fairly appalled that I've added one, but we like it that way. Crust or not, feel free to adopt this as your "house pie." It's best with peppermint ice cream. If you can't find peppermint ice cream, make your own by mixing crushed peppermint candies in vanilla ice cream.

INGREDIENTS

1 stick butter

2 squares (1 oz each) of unsweetened baking chocolate

1 cup sugar

2 eggs

¼ cup flour

1 tsp vanilla

Piecrust (*hint: It's fine to get the frozen ones in aluminum pans, but the piecrusts that you unroll and place in the pan are better and no more trouble if you own a pie pan. Find them with biscuits and cookie dough in the grocery store. Or make your own, page 63.*)

DIRECTIONS

In a double boiler over medium-high heat, melt butter and chocolate. (*hint: You can invent a double boiler by putting a small saucepan in a larger one that is filled about ⅓ of the way up with water.*)

Remove from heat to cool slightly.

Preheat oven to 350 degrees.

Mix sugar and eggs together. Add a little of the melted chocolate mixture to the egg mixture and stir together. (You do this to keep from having chocolate scrambled eggs, which happens if you add the eggs to the hot chocolate.)

Add all of egg mixture to the chocolate and stir to combine.

Mix in flour and vanilla.

Pour into piecrust and bake for about 30 minutes, until set.

Serves 6 to 8

Bonus Recipe: Fudge Cake

Change the ¼ cup flour to ½ cup and bake in an 8 × 8 pan, sprayed with baking spray (or buttered and floured) for same amount of time.

Icing

Melt 2 tbsp butter and a 2-oz square of unsweetened chocolate together in a microwave.

Mix with 1½ cups confectioners' sugar and enough milk to make icing. Add milk just a few spoons at a time. A little goes a long way.

Haystacks

INGREDIENTS

2 cups butterscotch chips (11 oz pkg)

2 tbsp peanut butter, plain or crunchy

5 or 6 oz pkg Chinese chow-mein noodles

1 cup salted peanuts

Optional: coarse salt

DIRECTIONS

Melt butterscotch chips in a large microwave-safe mixing bowl for about 2½ minutes, stopping to stir every 30 seconds.

Stir peanut butter into the melted butterscotch.

Add noodles and peanuts to the butterscotch mixture and stir to combine.

Drop the batter by the heaping tablespoon onto waxed paper and refrigerate until set, about 20 minutes.

Sprinkle haystack with a few grains of coarse salt if desired.

Makes about 30

Keep these in a sealed container or a zip-lock Baggie, and they are delicious for days!

Instant Chocolate Microwave Cake

I couldn't be the only person in the world who will staunchly declare that I'm not having dessert and an hour later crave something sweet so badly I can barely stand it. This is the cake for those moments. Plus, it's also kind of a fun recipe for impressing a friend with your cleverness!

INGREDIENTS

¼ cup flour

5 tbsp sugar

2 tbsp unsweetened cocoa powder

1 egg

3 tbsp milk

3 tbsp vegetable oil

⅛ tsp salt

½ tsp vanilla

DIRECTIONS

Whisk all ingredients in a medium bowl.

Pour into 2 large coffee mugs sprayed with cooking spray.

Microwave until puffed, about 2 minutes.

Eat as soon as it's cool enough.

Serves 2

Serving Suggestion: Good alone, but ice cream takes it to new heights.

No-Cook Apricot and Coconut Cookies

This delicious treat has a tart sweetness that makes it unique. If you're putting together a couple of desserts for a party, this recipe pairs well with chocolate, like the Super Easy Fudge, recipe page 163.

INGREDIENTS

12 oz pkg of dried apricots

1 tbsp lemon juice

2 cups coconut, 7 oz pkg (you can find this in the baking section)

½ cup sweetened condensed milk

½ cup confectioners' sugar for rolling cookies

DIRECTIONS

Put apricots in a food processor or a blender and grind up.

Mix ground apricots with lemon juice, coconut, and condensed milk.

Roll into small 1-inch balls, slightly smaller than a ping-pong ball.

Roll in confectioners' sugar.

Place on a baking sheet or a tray lined with wax paper to cool and dry out enough to store.

Keep covered in the refrigerator.

Makes about 25

One of Everything Fruit Pie Crumble

This recipe can practically be made with your eyes closed it's so simple. But once you do make it, you'll see why it's everyone's favorite.

INGREDIENTS

1 cup flour

1 cup sugar

1 egg

1 stick softened butter (can be softened in 10 seconds in a microwave)

1 can of your favorite fruit-pie filling: apple, cherry, or peach (can sizes differ, about 20 to 24 oz) *see note

DIRECTIONS

Preheat oven to 400 degrees.

To make the topping, mix the first four ingredients together in a large bowl using a fork, until it has a crumbly consistency.

Spray an 8 × 8 baking dish or pie pan with cooking spray.

Put pie filling in dish.

Add crumbled topping and bake until browned about 30 to 40 minutes.

It's delicious alone or with a little ice cream.

*You can certainly use fresh or frozen fruit, about 2 cups, peeled and chopped, if necessary. Add ¼ cup of sugar to the fruit.

Peach Mountain Rollups

This is my most requested dessert recipe. The first time I made Peach Mountain Rollups, I accidentally ended up serving it to a locally well-known chef. She dropped by to visit late one afternoon, and we asked her to stay for dinner because this is the South, and that's what we do. I was absolutely horrified to be making a dessert flavored with a soft drink, but it was already in the oven, and believe me, one taste and we were all hooked. She asked for the recipe to serve in her restaurant. Yeah, it is that good!

INGREDIENTS

2 cans refrigerated crescent rolls

4 ripe peaches, peeled and chopped *(hint: To peel a peach, drop in boiling water for about a minute, then run under cold water. The skin will slip right off.)* *see note

1 ⅓ cups sugar

2 sticks butter, melted *(hint: Melt in the microwave in a small bowl.)*

1 tsp apple-pie spice (you can substitute cinnamon or nutmeg or a combination)

12 oz can of Mountain Dew

DIRECTIONS

Preheat oven to 350 degrees.

Spray a 9 × 13 baking dish, or similar size casserole dish with cooking spray.

Unroll crescent rolls; separate into triangles.

Place a few peach pieces on the wide end of each triangle; roll up triangles around peaches, starting at wide end.

Place, point sides down, in prepared baking dish.

Stir together sugar, butter, and apple pie spice, and drizzle over rolls.

Pour Mountain Dew over rolls.

Bake for 45 minutes or until golden brown and bubbly.

This reheats very well.

Serves 8

* It's not the end of the world if you use frozen peaches. Thaw them a little so you can break them apart. It also works with peeled, cored, sliced apples.

Peanut Butter Cookies

This is the first cookie my son learned how to make, and it's still his favorite. If you've never entertained the idea of making a cookie in your life, this is a good place to begin. Once I was vacationing with friends in a rental house and decided to make these around 9:00 p.m. There was a lot of whining that it was too much trouble and would take too long. A fellow vacationer followed me into the kitchen trying to talk me out of it, but I had the batter mixed and ready to go before she could work up a really good argument. All she could say was, "That's it? Bake away!" I counted; she ate six.

INGREDIENTS

1 cup peanut butter, crunchy or smooth

1 cup sugar

1 egg

1 tsp baking soda

DIRECTIONS

Preheat oven to 350 degrees.

Mix all ingredients together.

Drop by tablespoon onto ungreased baking sheet.

Bake for 10 to 12 minutes.

Cool for a minute on baking sheet.

Remove to wax paper to cool completely and store in an airtight container *(hint: Large Baggies or disposable plastic containers work great.)*

Makes 24 to 30 cookies.

Suggestion: Add ½ cup of mini chocolate chips for a fun change.

Pots de Crème au Chocolate

(Fancy dessert made in the blender!)

This dessert is your little black dress (sorry, guys). It always makes a perfect statement, doesn't go out of style, and it never fails to make you feel quite elegant. It's perfect for entertaining because you prepare it even a day ahead of time and simply pop it in the fridge until serving time. I have a sizeable crush on pretty teacups, which are perfect for serving this dessert. They can be found very inexpensively at thrift stores and antique shops. It's even better if they don't match. But really, any old cup will do. No one will care once they taste this little bit of heaven!

INGREDIENTS

12 oz semisweet chocolate chips, or milk chocolate chips, or a combination of both

¼ cup sugar

4 eggs

1 cup whole milk or half & half

DIRECTIONS

Have 8 custard cups or small tea or coffee cups ready to fill.

Put chocolate, sugar, and eggs in a blender.

Blend at low speed pulsing until well mixed and the chocolate bits are pretty well broken up.

Heat the milk to boiling. *(hint: Heat in the microwave in a cup or bowl.)*

Pour the milk slowly into the blender while continuing to blend until smooth.

Pour into waiting cups and refrigerate until it sets up, about 4 hours.

Makes Eight 4-ounce cups

Serving suggestion: Top with whipped cream to make this really special. The whipped cream product in a can is actually real cream and tastes acceptable. Do not ever buy a frozen whipped topping product without feeling a little bad about it. Whipped Cream instructions appear with Banana Cream Pie, page 147, if you'd like to make your own.

Saltine Cookies

Terrible name, great cookie!

INGREDIENTS

Saltine crackers (enough to cover 9 × 13 pan—about one sleeve)

1 cup brown sugar

2 sticks butter

1½ cups semisweet chocolate chips

1 cup chopped pecans or toffee bits

DIRECTIONS

Preheat oven to 350 degrees.

Line rimmed baking sheet with foil, and spray with cooking spray.

Line prepared baking sheet with saltine crackers, salty side up, to cover completely.

In a medium saucepan, melt butter and add brown sugar.

Bring mixture to a boil, and boil for 3 minutes.

Pour mixture over the top of the saltines, making sure all are covered.

Place baking sheet in oven and bake for 5 minutes.

When you remove the baking sheet from oven, the brown-sugar mixture will be bubbly.

Sprinkle the chocolate chips over the brown-sugar mixture.

As chocolate melts, spread it to cover most of the crackers.

Sprinkle with chopped nuts or toffee bits.

Refrigerate for 1 hour.

Break into pieces.

Serves a bunch of people!

Super Easy Fudge

INGREDIENTS

1 can sweetened condensed milk (you can find this in the baking section)

3 cups (18 oz) semisweet chocolate chips

1 tbsp butter

1 tsp vanilla

DIRECTIONS

Lightly coat an 8 × 8 dish with cooking spray. *(hint: Line it with foil first for easy cutting and cleanup.)*

In a large microwave-safe bowl, melt chocolate and condensed milk together in the microwave, stirring every 30 seconds for about 2 minutes.

Remove when melted and stir in butter and vanilla.

Pour into prepared pan.

Cool until set, about 3 to 4 hours.

Cut into bite-sized squares.

Makes about 20 1-inch pieces

Suggestion: If you want to change this up a bit, here are some possible additions to the fudge before you pour it in the pan:

1 tsp instant espresso or coffee powder

20 mini-marshmallows

½ cup nuts

½ cup chopped dried fruit

Suggestion: This is a great gift! Wrap a few pieces in plastic wrap or wax paper and give them away as party favors. Tie the ends with ribbon for a festive touch! Everybody likes fudge.

The World's Best Cheesecake

INGREDIENTS

Crust

2 cups crushed graham crackers (you can buy graham-cracker crumbs in the baking section of the grocery store with flour and cake mixes)

1 stick melted butter *(hint: Melt in the microwave in a cup or bowl.)*

(hint: You can buy a perfectly acceptable premade crust in the baking section. The homemade ones do taste more buttery!)

Filling

3 (8 oz) pkg cream cheese, at room temperature

1½ cups sugar

5 eggs

3 tbsp lemon juice

Topping

2 cups of sour cream

½ cup sugar

1 tsp vanilla extract

DIRECTIONS

Preheat oven to 350 degrees.

Combine crust ingredients in a large bowl.

Mix well and press evenly across bottom and sides of a 10-inch springform pan or a cake pan.

Combine cream cheese and sugar in a large bowl. An electric mixer will make this much easier.

Add eggs beating thoroughly.

Beat in the lemon juice.

Pour filling into crust. *(hint: Line a baking sheet with foil and put cheesecake on it to bake in case any filling spills over.)*

Bake for 45 minutes without opening the oven door.

Remove cheesecake and reduce oven heat to 300 degrees.

Mix topping ingredients in a medium bowl and spread over cheesecake.

Return to oven and bake 15 minutes longer.

Cool to room temperature and refrigerate until cold.

Serves 10

Suggestion: Cheesecake is wonderful all by itself, but there are lots of great cheesecake toppings if you want to add a special touch. Fresh fruit is always perfect—maybe sliced strawberries or peaches. Other berries are good as well—raspberries and blueberries are delicious. In a pinch you could use a canned-fruit pie filling like cherry or apple. Or you could go all out and make the Chocolate or Caramel Sauce, pages 148.

Very Easy Chocolate Turnovers

When I went to France I was a hungry college student always looking for a food bargain. We were staying near Versailles, where there was a bakery that had this marvelous pastry with a French name that I don't remember, but it doesn't matter since we renamed it "chocolate in the middle bread" because, well, that's what it was. And because it was cheap and thoroughly delicious, I ate lots of it. This recipe reminds me of chocolate bread. It should probably have a better name too. Make it, taste it, and see what you come up with!

INGREDIENTS

1 box puff pastry (2 sheets in a box)

Chocolate candy bar that can be broken into 12 squares, your choice—milk, dark, with or without nuts

1 egg, beaten for egg wash *see note

2 tbsp sugar

DIRECTIONS

Thaw puff-pastry dough.

Lightly spray a baking sheet with cooking spray.

Roll out pastry a little to flatten. Cut into squares about 3 inches each. Use the folds in pastry as a guide to get 12 squares. Each sheet should yield 6 squares.

Put one piece of chocolate in each square and fold over into a triangle shape.

Press edges together to seal. The tines of a fork work well for this.

Put squares on a prepared baking sheet.

Brush with egg wash and sprinkle with the sugar.

Put in the freezer while you preheat oven to 400 degrees.

Bake 10 to 15 minutes until puffed and golden.

Makes 12 pastries

* *To make an egg wash, you just beat eggs and brush the mixture on the pastry.

NOTES

Stocking a New Kitchen

This is the list we used to stock the kitchen when my son moved into his new and completely bare apartment. It reflects a couple of additions of items he found necessary after moving in. We personalized his list by adding his favorites—like orange juice, deli meats, ground beef, and ice cream. He has a wish list for some appliances he would like to add later. We also scoured Goodwill and thrift shops for an iron skillet and some great casserole dishes. Definitely use this list as a starting point, and then make it your own. Happy cooking!

Pots and Pans: 2 nonstick skillets, small and large; small and large saucepan with lids—one could be a Dutch Oven; baking sheet; pie pan; 2 cake pans; 2 casserole dishes: 9 × 13 and 8 × 8; 2 mixing bowls

Utensils: small and large spatulas, plastic flexible spatula, tongs, 2 large spoons for stirring (1 slotted), whisk, cheese grater, 3 good knives—small, medium, and large—set of measuring cups, measuring spoons, cutting board, colander, vegetable peeler, can opener, corkscrew bottle opener, whisk, rolling pin

Small Appliances: mixer (stand or hand-held), blender, Crock-Pot, coffee pot, food processor

Staples for Cooking: salt and pepper, flour, cornmeal, baking mix, sugar, brown sugar, confectioners' sugar, baking soda, baking powder, olive oil, canola oil, cooking spray, hot sauce, soy sauce, vinegar, canned soups of your choice, bouillon cubes—beef, chicken, and vegetable, cocoa powder, chocolate chips, vanilla, nuts, Ramen noodles, oatmeal, popcorn, coffee, and tea

12 Essential Spices: basil, chili powder, cinnamon, cumin, curry powder, garlic salt or powder, nutmeg, oregano, paprika, red pepper flakes, sage, thyme

Refrigerator: butter, milk, eggs, bread, mayonnaise, mustard, ketchup, salsa, pickles, sour cream, jelly or jam, bread, cheeses of choice, proteins of choice

Fruit and Veggie Drawer of Refrigerator: potatoes, onions, carrots, apples, citrus fruit, lemons, spinach, lettuce, plus other fruits and vegetables you like

Freezer: frozen vegetables, frozen fruit, chicken breasts, frozen yogurt or ice cream, foods you like for convenience—like whole grain waffles, pizzas, and burritos

Storage and Cooking: plastic wrap, large- and small-zip Baggies, waxed paper, aluminum foil, plastic containers

CPSIA information can be obtained
at www.ICGtesting.com
Printed in the USA
LVOW06*1907061117
555268LV00011B/19/P

9 781633 934771